Student Guide
to
The Writing Program
at
The University of Tulsa

Fifth Edition

Fountainhead Press

As a textbook publisher, we are faced with enormous environmental issues due the large amount of paper contained in our print products. Since our inception in 2002, we have worked diligently to be as eco-friendly as possible.

Our "green" initiatives include:

Electronic Products
We deliver products in non-paper form whenever possible. This includes pdf downloadables, flash drives, & CD's.

Electronic Samples
We use a new electronic sampling system, called Xample. Instructor samples are sent via a personalized web page that links to pdf downloads.

FSC Certified Printers
All of our Printers are certified by the Forest Service Council which promotes environmentally and socially responsible management of the world's forests. This program allows consumer groups, individual consumers and businesses to work together hand in hand to promote responsible use of the world's forests as a renewable and sustainable resource.

Recycled Paper
Almost all of our products are printed on a minimum of 10-30% post consumer waste recycled paper.

Support of Green Causes
When we do print, we donate a portion of our revenue to Green causes. Listed below are a few of the organizations that have received donations from Fountainhead Press. We welcome your feedback and suggestions for contributions, as we are always searching for worthy initiatives.

Rainforest 2 Reef
Environmental Working Group

Cover design: Doris Bruey, DB Graphic Design Services

Copyright 2010 by G. Matthew Jenkins

"First-Year Composition as an Introduction to Academic Discourse," copyright 1999 by the National Council of Teachers of English. Reprinted with permission.

Books may be purchased for educational purposes.

For information, please call or write:

1-800-586-0330

Fountainhead Press
2140 E. Southlake Blvd. Ste L #816
Southlake, TX 76092

Web site: www.fountainheadpress.com
Email: customerservice@fountainheadpress.com

Fifth Edition

ISBN 978-1-59871-409-8

Printed in the United States of America

Student Guide to The University of Tulsa Writing Program

Table of Contents

PREFACE

The purpose of this Guide is to acclimate students to the requirements, policies, and procedures of required writing courses at the University of Tulsa. Although this Guide is mainly written for first-year students, you will here find information and documents—such as the definition of "plagiarism" and the TU Plagiarism Statement Acknowledgement Form—that will be used and useful for the rest of your college career. *Please keep this Guide until you have finished all writing requirements.* This Guide also offers useful tips, hints, and strategies to help you successfully navigate the University's writing courses and, better yet, to improve your writing overall as you prepare for your life and career after college.

Many people contributed to this Guide, and I would like to extend my gratitude to them for their efforts. First and foremost, I'd like to thank the original members of the Writing Program Guide Committee: Gina Berend-Perkins, Joshua Brazee, Karen Dutoi, Matthew Perry, and Dane Spencer. Composing various parts of this document, they devoted many hours to this project that will benefit not only them and their students but everyone in the Program. Many thanks to Felix Frazier and his staff at Fountainhead Press for their design and publishing expertise. Also, thank you to Mrs. Sandy Vice, Departmental Assistant, who guides this Program administratively and spiritually and serves as our ambassador to the world. To Lars Engle, Chair of the English Department, and Tom Benediktson, Dean of the College of Arts & Sciences whose moral and financial support is much appreciated. Notably, I would like to thank the current Writing Program Guide Committee that was responsible for the changes to previous editions: Jami Barnett, Sara Beam, Gina Berend-Perkins, Julie Bishop, Jennifer Chapman, Samantha Extance, Michael Griffin, Tabitha Hibbs, Ashley Johnson, Katherine McGee, Dane Spencer, Andy Trevathan, and Barbara Woodfin.

Last but certainly not least, I would also like to thank each and every member of the Writing Program for his or her hard work and dedication. Their energy makes this Program work.

G. Matthew Jenkins
Director of the Writing Program
The University of Tulsa

INTRODUCTION

We, the faculty and staff of the University of Tulsa Writing Program, understand that starting college can be an intimidating rite of passage not only because we've seen many students come through our doors but because we've been there ourselves. We also hear from many of our students things like "English is not my best subject," "I'm a lousy writer," or "I'm only taking this class because I have to." But we feel that written communication is such an important skill, no matter what you choose to do with your degree, that we will go to almost any length to fill you with the passion for writing that urged us to become writing teachers. Falling short of that, we aim to equip you with the tools and tricks you will need to be successful throughout your college career and life, not just at writing, but at thinking critically about the world and your place in it.

This guide is the first step towards acquiring those skills. In it, you will find course descriptions and requirements, necessary documents, useful hints, and other materials that we hope will make your transition into college writing much easier. *We recommend that you keep this guide, along with your writing handbook, throughout your college career.* It contains information and documents that you will use in each of your writing classes.

What Is the Point?

One of the main purposes of first-year writing is to make you aware that writing is not an isolated activity. When you write, you are participating in a long, rich tradition that dates back thousands of years. When you write, you are also drawing upon strategies and structures of language that have been adopted and adapted by language users across cultures, time periods, and political boundaries. When you write, you negotiate those traditions of language use with your own position as a writer from a particular time and place with its own conventions, expectations, and language styles. Also, when you write, you integrate, consciously or not, the words of others from what you have read and researched, in addition to the responses of others from your peers to your professors to the audience you imagine in your head. And lastly, when you write, you not only express yourself as an individual but you pay homage and respect, as well as bear a greater responsibility, to something larger than yourself. It should be no wonder, then, why some authors and teachers see writing almost as a sacred activity.

With this greater awareness, you will be able to make powerful and effective choices in expressing yourself to whatever audience in whatever situation you may find yourself. Through practice—reading, writing, and revision—you will hone your skills and continue a process of improvement that will continue for the rest of your life. You see, there is no such thing as "perfect" writing—even an Ernest Hemingway or Toni Morrison continually strives to improve his or her writing. Keeping that in mind, we will work together to improve our writing. You may not realize this, but because learning how to write is a life-long process, we as writing teachers often learn as much about writing from teaching you as you do from taking our class.

Because writing is always larger than the individual, this course will help you become part of a particular academic conversation, or "discourse community," to which you will add your unique perspective with the goal of broadening our knowledge of the world. Since knowledge is created in academia through writing, writing is a primary way that you will be learning new things as you progress through school. By becoming part of one specific discourse community in your writing course, you will acquire skills that will allow you to navigate and become part of any discourse community.

Lastly, this course aims to acclimate you to the art and expectations of academic writing, which is scholarly writing in the university that may take the form of argument, narrative, reports, proposals, or some other conventional form. To quote M.J. Braun and Sarah Prineas, two experts in composition studies whose essay, "The Process of Research," is reproduced here: "Our purpose is to arm young scholars with the frameworks they will need to be able to assess scholarship critically, even from their non-expert positions within the university" (571). Although your composition course may focus on a particular discipline, such as literary studies, or topic, such as "The Construction of Gender in Law and Medicine," it will offer you skills that are transferable to any discourse community.

What Is Writing? Better Yet, What Is *Good* Writing?

Over the past 2500 years, there have been many different answers to those questions, and they have become even more hotly debated since modern first-year writing classes became standard fare in colleges in the 1960s. From a rhetorical point of view, writing is a form of expression or communication that involves a writer, a text, a context (situation, tradition, debate, etc), and an audience (aka discourse community, etc.). The variations in the definition of "writing" arise in the meaning and significance of each of those elements.

A much more practical question, and one that often befuddles first-year writing students, is what makes for *good* writing. It is true that each instructor has his or her own particular ideas on how to achieve good writing and may even have an entirely original definition of "writing" itself. These apparent differences might make it seem to you that "every teacher wants something different." Despite this rigorous academic debate, most teachers of writing will agree on what constitutes *good* writing, even if their philosophies of writing differ widely. In short, good writing is found in a text that achieves its purpose with a particular audience through effective choices involving organization and style. Your "achievement" and "effectiveness" will be measured against a standard set of criteria. We work as a department to achieve a consensus on our standards and definitions and to continually keep up with the latest research developments in how to best teach good writing.

To insure that your writing is "good enough," or proficient, for your career at TU, the Writing Program employs a review of a portfolio, a collection of your best writing, that you produce in ENGL 1033. This Guide, therefore, includes the criteria, procedures, and requirements by which your writing will be assessed through the review (see the "ENGL 1033 Portfolio Assessment System" section of this Guide for more information).

What Does It Take to Pass This Class?

We know that you are concerned about your grade and want to get the highest marks that you can on your work in your writing class. However, as instructors, we would prefer you to focus on making your writing better first and then letting the grade follow from that. You may be thinking, "Sure, that's easy for you to say," but we ask that you trust the fact that we, as writing teachers, want you to succeed in your writing courses as much as you do. Our goal is not to fail everyone who makes a grammar mistake, but neither is it to define successful writing as making an "A." Instead, we want students to leave our courses as confident writers prepared to meet the challenges of college-level writing and thinking.

When you talk to your friends and peers who are in other sections of first-year writing courses, you will notice that there are a wide variety of approaches taken by instructors. Each instructor will choose methods that best fit his or her own style and philosophy, as well as ones tailored to meet the needs of individual classes or individual students. While your instructor may make lecture-style presentations occasionally, you may also encounter class discussion of readings, small group work, in-class revision and writing exercises, online writing and communication, library visits, grammar workshops, and a myriad other activities. As the old saying goes, there are many roads to the same destination.

Regardless of your instructor's approach, you will also notice a difference between high school and college-level proficiency. As you probably have anticipated, your college writing classes will expect much more out of you than did your high school English classes. Even if you were considered a "good writer" in high school, you will still need to build off that foundation and work to improve your writing so that you may meet our rigorous standards. These standards, outlined in several of the sections of this Guide, are designed to help you meet the demands of all of your college courses, not just your writing courses.

Thus, our Program emphasizes writing as a *process* just as much as a product. To that end, your first-year writing course will involve revision, often of multiple drafts, and feedback from peers and your instructor. The relatively small size of writing courses at TU facilitates this kind of interaction, which has been proven to be the most effective way to improve student writing.

In addition to writing, reading and research may be very important parts of your class. Studies show that good readers are good writers, so you will learn to analyze texts in a way that will help you improve your own rhetorical and stylistic choices. Doing research, which is a special kind of reading, will help you learn that all writing is, in a way, a response to other texts that make up a context integral to a specific discourse community. By reading, analyzing, and responding to the texts of others in a discourse community, you will become a better writer and a better thinker.

How Much Work Will This Class Be?
This is one of the questions that students most often ask about first-year writing courses. Although the exact answer to it depends upon the individual instructor, each course in the program has set minimum requirements that often include number of total pages of revised writing, number of out-of-class essays, in-class writing assignments, or other kinds of activities. For example, you may be required to meet with your professor in a conference or attend a required weekly workshop for your course.

Because writing by its nature is labor-intensive, expect to spend more time on the work for your writing classes than you might for other introductory classes. A rule of thumb is 2-4 hours of work out of class for every hour your class meets per week. For example, if the class is a 3 hour class, you can expect to spend around 9 hours outside of class (Wilson). Of course, the time commitment will vary depending upon the kind of reading and writing you are doing at a particular time of the semester—for instance, expect to spend more time on this course when you are working on a research project.

Things to Think About
The following tips come from years of experience with what works and what doesn't. Many of the suggestions come from students themselves who wish that somebody had told them these things when they started college:
- Be prepared each class day with any reading, homework, or assignments due.
- Keep up with assignments. Look at your syllabus and schedule often so that you can plan ahead for what you need to do and when it is due. If you miss class, be sure to get notes from a classmate.
- *Don't wait until the night before.* This is one of the reasons many instructors require drafts or other preliminary steps of an essay—so that you can get suggestions to improve the essay before it is assessed. If you miss class, fail to bring a draft, or write an inferior draft, you will miss out on the opportunity to receive the best feedback you can get to help you succeed on an essay.
- Take in-class assignments and/or portfolio assessments as seriously as you would an out-of-class research paper.
- Seek help from your instructor outside of class; solicit feedback from peers (while always doing your own work); and take advantage of your college's writing resources, which include a writing center staffed with helpful consultants.

- Practice! Use every opportunity you can to read and write—don't just read and write for school work. Write letters, emails, instant messages, or keep a journal. Subscribe to a magazine or newspaper that fits your lifestyle or political interest or just read the campus rag. More importantly, read things that challenge you—editorials, novels, and professional writings—so that you can learn from the best and pick up new tricks of the trade.

For more information on how to succeed in all of your college classes, not just writing, see the University of Tulsa "Handbook: College Experience" in the Works Cited (Wilson). It outlines expectations, study strategies, and useful tips for getting the results you want from your education.

Issues for Non-Native Students

If English is not your first language, you may face some particular challenges as you start your college career. First of all, you should know that even most native speakers of English have a hard time with writing because it is a very difficult skill to master even when you know the language.

However, your writing instructor can help you with those problems—such as grammatical rules and cultural conventions—that native speakers take for granted. Your teacher can identify any language areas in which you need extra work and can direct you to resources on campus that will help you address those problems. However, teachers can only go so far; it is your responsibility to seek out any extra help that may be required for you to meet the rigorous standards that all college writers have to meet. Even after seeking help on your writing, you must finally make the decisions of how best to do your own work.

THE UNIVERSITY OF TULSA WRITING PROGRAM

OVERVIEW OF PROGRAM, COURSE DESCRIPTIONS AND SEQUENCE

The University Writing Program, which serves most students at the University of Tulsa, is part of and housed in the English Department. Designed to position writing as central within the university curriculum, the current program emphasizes rigorous courses that introduce students to the conventions of academic writing and then assists them in moving into writing-intensive courses taught by faculty members from a variety of departments and colleges.

Summary of University Writing Requirements

When you enrolled at TU, you were required to designate a College affiliation based on your sense of which one best fit the course of study you might pursue. This designation is important because it will determine which sequence of writing courses you will follow. All TU students are required to take at least two writing courses. Here is a summary of that sequence divided by College affiliation:

Students in Arts and Sciences

ENGL 1004 (if required) ➜ ENGL 1033 ➜ FS 1973.

Students in Business and Engineering

ENGL 1004 (if required) ➜ ENGL 1033 ➜ ENGL 3003.

If you need more practice in the fundamentals of writing (as evidenced by your test scores and performance on a diagnostic writing test), you will be enrolled in ENGL 1004, "Introduction to College Writing," a course designed to provide review and practice in basic skills. In addition, while all writing courses seek to address the needs of non-native speakers, a few sections of ENGL 1004 and ENGL 1033, "Exposition and Argumentation," are designated specifically for non-native speaking students.

The majority of first-semester students enroll in ENGL 1033, "Exposition and Argumentation," a course in the process, conventions, and production of academic writing. You will learn in this course to refine and develop arguments, while gaining knowledge of the fundamentals of library research and online resources.

Following 1033, if you are in the College of Arts and Sciences, you enroll in a First Seminar taught by a faculty member from a diverse group of departments and designed to engage small groups of students in close study of a focused topic. A major aspect of the course is the completion of several writing assignments in which careful and thorough revision is required. Course topics from past semesters include "Exploring the Neanderthals," "20th Century Jazz Masters," "Reading and Writing Spiritual Autobiography," "Mark Twain's America," and "Creativity in the Arts."

If you are in the College of Business and the College of Engineering and Natural Sciences, you will follow ENGL 1033 with ENGL 3003, "Writing for the Professions," a course designed to assist students in developing skills in written and oral communication for business and engineering professions.

If you change colleges during your career, it could affect the writing requirements you must fulfill. Implementation practices may vary according to degree programs in individual Colleges, especially in the Colleges of Business and Engineering/Natural Sciences. You should consult advisors in the specific college to which you are transferring. Generally, students transferring into the College of Arts and Sciences will be advised to enroll in FS 1973, while students in the Colleges of Business and Engineering/Natural Sciences will be advised to enroll in ENGL 3003 when they have reached junior standing.

All students at the University are invited to use the Writing Center located in Chapman Hall (631-3131). Staffed by graduate assistants in English, the center offers consultations in individual or group sessions to help you develop and improve your writing skills. (See "Campus Writing Resources" section for more information).

The University Writing Program serves as a center for writing-across-the-curriculum activities at the University. The staff of the Writing Program is available to consult with faculty members in all departments about integrating manageable and effective writing assignments in their courses.

Course Descriptions in Brief

English 1004, "Introduction to College Writing." This course provides students with review and practice in the fundamentals of college writing, including organization, paragraph development, basic research skills, logic, and mechanics. Class meets three hours per week; lab meets one hour per week. Some sections designated for non-native speakers of English. Staffing: Teaching Assistants and faculty in English. Enrollment: 15

English 1033, "Exposition and Argumentation." This course emphasizes the process, conventions, and production of academic writing; refining and developing an argument; and library research and documentation of sources. Thorough and frequent revision is integral to the preparation of all written work. Some sections designated for non-native speakers of English. Pre-requisite: English 1004 or satisfactory placement and diagnostic test scores; required for all students, regardless of College. Staffing: Teaching Assistants and faculty in English. Enrollment: 18

First Seminar 1973, Writing Intensive Seminar. Designed by individual faculty members in the College of Arts & Sciences and coordinated by the Writing Program Director, the seminars are discipline-centered courses that stress writing as the primary way in which students demonstrate their learning of the material. Students enrolled in the course are expected to produce 20-25 pages of revised writing during the course of the semester in a variety of written assignments. Pre-requisite: English 1033, advanced placement credit, or equivalent; required for students in Arts and Sciences. Staffing: Arts & Sciences faculty sometimes with assistance from Teaching Assistants in English. Enrollment: 17

English 3003, "Writing for the Professions." This course adapts principles of effective writing to situations encountered in business and engineering professions (including nursing and biology). Letters, resumes, and a full investigative report in the student's discipline are required. Pre-requisites: Junior standing and English 1033; required for students in the College of Business and the College of Engineering and Natural Sciences, depending on program. Staffing: Teaching Assistants and faculty in English. Enrollment: 15.

Placement in ENGL 1004 and 1033

Test scores are used for preliminary placement into writing courses. Students who score 20 and below on the verbal sections of the ACT or 490 and below on the SAT I will be enrolled in ENGL 1004. International students without ACT or equivalent test scores may be placed in non-native sections of ENGL 1004, on the basis of interviews with their advisors. Students with ACT verbal scores of 21 and above and SAT I equivalents of 500 and above will be placed in ENGL 1033.

Students in the College of Business Administration seeking either a B.S.B.A. or a B.S.I.B.L. degree must earn a grade of C or above to pass ENGL 1033 and ENGL 3003. All other students may earn a grade of D or above to pass these courses.

In all cases, your placement is not finally determined in any course until the evaluation of a diagnostic essay, which is administered during the first week of class meetings of ENGL 1004 and 1033. You will be advised by your instructors and the Director of the Writing Program if the initial placement seems inappropriate. If you have a question about placement in a writing course, you should consult the Director of the Writing Program or your advisor.

Advanced Placement Credit

Students who score a 4 on the English-Language and Composition Exam may receive three hours credit and be excused from enrolling in ENGL 1033, and those who score a 4 on the English-Literature and Composition Exam may receive three hours credit for ENGL 1053, "The Narrative Imagination."

International Baccalaureate Examination Credit

Students who score a 5 on the English HL Exam may receive six hours credit and be excused from enrolling in ENGL 1033 and ENGL 1053, "The Narrative Imagination." Students who score a 5 on the English SL Exam may receive three hours credit for ENGL 1053.

Transfer of Credits

In general, the transcripts of students who transfer from accredited institutions are evaluated by The Director of the Writing Program and other advisors according to the following guidelines:

- Students who transfer three hours of basic or developmental writing from an accredited institution and earn a grade of C or above will receive a credit for ENGL 1004.
- Students who transfer six hours of freshman composition (excluding basic or developmental writing) or the second course (of three hours credit) of a two-course freshman composition sequence from an accredited institution and earn a grade of C or above will receive credit for ENGL 1033.

The University of Tulsa Writing Program

ENGL 1033 Portfolio Assessment System

Like many colleges and universities across the country, The University of Tulsa Writing Program uses a portfolio-style assessment system to determine if you have met the basic requirements of first-year writing (see the "Overview" section of this Guide). Without these basic writing skills, you may have difficulty negotiating the more rigorous writing requirements of your other courses, particularly the ones in your major field. In ENGL 1033, the first semester writing course for most students, you will gather a sample of your writing from the course and submit it in an official folder to be read by a committee of English instructors, consultants, and administrators. The committee assesses whether you have met the basic requirements, and your instructor notifies you of the results. (Please note: your portfolio will not be returned to you but is kept on file in the Writing Program office as a record of your achievement).

Although this process sounds very mysterious, it is actually quite carefully designed to insure the most objective, consistent, and fair evaluation possible of your writing. There are four ways in which the portfolio system attempts to meet that goal: First, the portfolio rewards hard work by allowing you to revise your essays several times before submitting them. Second, you will select a sample of your *best* writing from the semester, so, in a sense, you get to put your best foot forward. Third, you will remove your name from the papers so that the committee will be reading your work anonymously, as free as possible from factors—such as knowledge of learning style, gender, ethnicity, or personality—that might influence grading. Lastly, your instructor will not be part of the committee that assesses your work.

The criteria the committee will use to grade your portfolio is spelled out in detail in this section of the Guide. These criteria were painstakingly designed by the Writing Program as a whole and reflect a consensus as to what counts as proficient writing at The University of Tulsa. In short, the criteria are rhetorically based. That is, they assess the writer's ability to argue a particular position and to make controlled and effective choices with language in order to achieve that argument's purpose with a certain audience, or discourse community. The criteria are periodically revised to reflect recent advancements in the field of Composition and Rhetoric, and the Writing Program meets regularly to practice thorough, consistent, and fair application of the criteria to student writing.

In ENGL 1033, your portfolio will be assessed twice—once at midterm in a sort of "dry run" to give you a sense of where you stand in relation to the criteria and again toward the end of the term. After each review, your instructor will inform you of the results and what it will mean for your grade in the course. *Please note: If you fail the final portfolio review, you will be required to retake the course.*

Other details, such as due dates, portfolio contents, exact scoring criteria, and other instructions, can be found in the section that follows. Please read it carefully so that you will be prepared for portfolio assessment—it would be a shame for you to fail the review simply because you did not follow instructions. Our goal as a Writing Program is not to try to "trip you up" or "make you fail" by using a portfolio review—in fact, the passing rate of portfolio review since 2000 has been around 90%. Instead, we strive to make sure that you are proficient writers so that you can meet the demands of college-level writing. To help you achieve that goal, we offer you thorough practice, one-on-one attention, regular feedback, and excellent instruction.

UNIVERSITY OF TULSA WRITING PROGRAM

INSTRUCTIONS FOR COMPILING YOUR ENGL 1033 <u>MID-TERM</u> WRITING PORTFOLIO

Use these general guidelines as you prepare your mid-term writing portfolio for your ENGL 1033 class. Although this handout is designed to help you through the process of compiling the portfolio, feel free to ask your instructor for more detailed explanations on any aspect of the process.

Mid-Term Portfolio Due Date
Please consult your course syllabus for the midterm portfolio due date.
Please note: NO LATE PORTFOLIOS WILL BE ACCEPTED.

Mid-Term Portfolio Contents
Your portfolio, which will be evaluated on a pass/fail basis, should include an introductory reflective essay written according to the directions below, one of your unrevised in-class essays, and one revised essay. The revised essay must be either (1) a short essay (3-4 pages) using the textbook as a source or (2) a longer essay (5-6 pages) using three to four sources.

Remember that you have a better chance of passing the portfolio evaluation if you revise your papers further—perhaps even *several* times during the semester—using your instructor and the Writing Center as resources during the process. When you compile your mid-term portfolio, make sure to include *all* of the following items because incomplete portfolios do not pass:

Mid-Term Portfolio Contents Checklist
❑ Introductory reflective essay (1 page) ❑ One unrevised in-class essay ❑ One revised 3- to 4-page paper (with the course textbook as a source) or one revised 5- to 6-page paper (using at least 3 academic sources in addition to the primary text)

Academic Sources
Academic sources are defined by the Writing Program as peer-reviewed articles or books from a particular discipline or discourse community (see section "The Research Process" for more information). Regardless of whether they come from print or electronic resources, these books and articles typically have extensive bibliographies and/or footnoted sources. Acceptable academic sources include journals like the *James Joyce Quarterly* or *Tulsa Studies in Women's Literature* and books like Lars Engle's *Shakespearean Pragmatism* or Holly Laird's *Women Coauthors*. Keep in mind that many web pages that you may find through Google or another internet search engine are most likely not academic (See the Library Resource section of this Guide for more information on finding and using adequate electronic resources). Not having the required number of academic sources is grounds for portfolio failure.

Introductory Reflective Essay

The introductory reflective essay will be placed first in your portfolio and will be among the most important papers that you write all semester. Besides introducing the other papers in the portfolio, your introductory essay presents an argument to convince the Portfolio Committee that your portfolio meets the requirements and objectives of the course. Remember that first impressions are important, and the essay will be the first piece of your writing that portfolio readers see. As Nedra Reynolds writes in *Portfolio Keeping*, portfolio readers will be looking for "writers who are insightful, conscientious, and engaged in learning" (45). Your essays should have clear organizational structures, each including an introduction, a body (in which you provide supporting evidence of your claims about your work), and a conclusion that leads readers into the rest of your portfolio.

Your introductory reflective essay *must include all* of the following elements:
- ❑ Paragraph structure with thesis, body, and conclusion
- ❑ Discussion of each item chosen for inclusion in the portfolio
- ❑ Thoughtful reflection about your writing process
- ❑ Assessment of the strengths and weaknesses of your own work
- ❑ Concrete examples from your own writing for support

You will probably want to use *some* of the following suggestions adapted from *Portfolio Keeping*, but remember that you are *not* expected to use all of them:
- Do not merely summarize your papers—the reviewers will be reading them—but instead draw on them for evidence to support your points about what you have learned and what you still need to work on.
- Discuss which paper you consider your best one and explain why.
- Explain in detail the revisions that you have made to one or more of the pieces, pointing out particular improvements that you want readers to notice.
- Indicate the particular strengths of each item in the portfolio.
- Take the reader through the process that you followed in writing one or more of the papers.
- Explain what your portfolio as a whole demonstrates about you as a writer, student, researcher, or critical thinker.
- Acknowledge your weaknesses as a writer but show how you have worked—and are continuing to work—to overcome them.
- Acknowledge how responses from your classmates and instructor have influenced the writing included in your portfolio.
- Reflect on what you have learned about writing through reading, writing, and discussion.
- Identify particular features or patterns of your writing process.
- Indicate which writing strategies worked well for you and which worked less well, explaining why you believe this to be the case.
- Discuss which piece of writing you enjoyed most or least and explain why.

(Reynolds 44)

Your introductory reflective essay should be at least one typed page long.

Preparing Your Mid-Term Portfolio

Submit your portfolio to your instructor in the official portfolio folder that came with this guide. Replacements for lost folders are available in the university bookstore in ACAC. Once you have obtained a folder, insert the required materials in the right order. The introductory reflective essay should be first, but you should organize the other papers strategically to showcase your writing ability. If portfolio readers read your best essay last, for example, they may feel more positively about your portfolio as a whole than they would if they read a less successful paper last.

Remove your name and your instructor's name from each of the papers you include in your portfolio, otherwise you may fail review. Instead of your name, include your **complete TU student ID number** along with the course number *and* section number on each page of each essay and on the outside of the portfolio folder.

Mid-Term Portfolio Preparation Checklist

- ❏ Use official portfolio folder
- ❏ Remove student and instructor names
- ❏ Place ID number on all papers and on folder
- ❏ Include course number *and* section number on all papers and on folder
- ❏ Place introductory essay first
    - ❏ Essay structure with introduction, body, and conclusion
    - ❏ Discussion of each item chosen for inclusion in the portfolio
    - ❏ Evidence of thoughtful reflection about your writing process
    - ❏ Evidence of ability to assess the strengths and weaknesses of your own work
- ❏ Include all required items
    - ❏ Introductory reflective essay (1 page)
    - ❏ One unrevised in-class essay
    - ❏ Either one revised 3- to 4-page paper (with the course textbook as a source) or one revised 5- to 6-page paper (using at least 3 academic sources in addition to the primary text)
- ❏ Make sure all essays meet minimum page and source number requirements

Mid-Term Portfolio Scoring Criteria

Your portfolio will be scored by a committee of reviewers from the Writing Program according to the following criteria. The following chart closely resembles the scoring sheet that committee reviewers will be using to assess your work.

Midterm Portfolio Scoring Sheet

Course Section Number: _____ Student ID Number: _____ Reviewer Number: _____

A passing portfolio should demonstrate that the student has a basic mastery of the objectives of ENGL 1033 and should meet the following criteria. Reviewers may evaluate each portfolio holistically or analytically, weighing its components equally.

If a portfolio does not contain one of the following elements below, please check "fail" at the bottom of this sheet.

Yes	No	
☐	☐	Introductory essay
☐	☐	In-class writing
☐	☐	One essay with at least three full pages and a class reading documented as source
☐	☐	Works cited page(s) for previous essay

After a thorough reading of student work, please check the following elements as they apply. Portfolio exhibits:

Yes	No	
☐	☐	Arguments generally unified around a central idea or thesis
☐	☐	Topics adequately narrow for length of essays
☐	☐	Overall content that demonstrates critical thinking (apply, extend, critique)
☐	☐	Appropriate rhetorical choices considering audience, purpose, tone, and point of view
☐	☐	Introductions that attempt to justify and contextualize thesis within a discourse community; conclusions that connect argument to larger concerns of that community
☐	☐	Development and organization of points logically and coherently
☐	☐	Adequate use of detail and evidence to support points
☐	☐	Effective integration and responsible MLA documentation of required no. of textual sources
☐	☐	Attempts to convey style and voice (diction, figures of speech, syntax, sentence variety, etc)
☐	☐	Awareness of conventions of Standard American English so that errors do not obscure content

---

Please include any written comments on the reverse of this form. Reviewer recommends that this portfolio:

Pass	Fail	
☐	☐	Portfolio Score

PORTFOLIOS THAT CONTAIN PAPERS THAT DO NOT MEET THE MINIMUM PAGE RE-QUIREMENTS WILL FAIL. So please make sure that all papers meet the requirements.

The following rubric gives a general, or holistic, description of the qualities of passing and failing portfolios. Reviewers will decide which category best fits with a particular portfolio in deciding results. This rubric supplements the analytical rubric (above) that divides portfolio assessment into it elements, each one reflecting an objective of the course as stated in the syllabus.

A <u>passing portfolio</u> should demonstrate that the student has a basic mastery of the objectives of ENGL 1033 and should fit this profile in most aspects. As a whole, the passing portfolio shows that the student can narrow a topic adequately for the given length of an essay and that he or she can stay on topic with only a few minor digressions. The contents of the portfolio also reveal that the student has made rhetorical choices (tone, point of view, genre, etc.) appropriate to the audience and purpose of the piece (both of which should be apparently implied in the argument). Introductions attempt to justify why the argument is necessary for a particular discourse community and place the thesis in a relevant context, even if the student may not completely understand that community. Overall, the content of the portfolio makes attempts at critical thinking, whether that be application, extension, or critique (aka "reading against the grain") of a text or discourse community. Concerning paragraphs, all major points are unified with the central idea or thesis and are supported with adequate, concrete textual evidence. Evidence is often but not always related back to the thesis coherently (transitions, repetition, synonyms, etc.) and is organized and developed in a consistent and sustained, if sometimes sloppy, manner (using modes of development—definition, cause/effect, proposal, illustration, etc.; with a logical order—chronological, emphatic, spatial, etc.). Pieces of writing usually integrate textual sources fairly, accurately, and effectively with only some formal mistakes or potential misreadings. Portfolio should not fail for misreadings alone. Citation style may not be completely accurate but should demonstrate an attempt to credit sources when necessary to avoid plagiarism. Conclusion may summarize main points but should also attempt to spell out ramifications of the argument for a particular discourse community. On the sentence level, the portfolio should reveal attempts to convey style and voice through diction, syntax, figurative language, etc. on at least a minimal level. Passing portfolios also exhibit control of conventions of Standard American English so that errors do not overly inhibit content of argument. There is no set limit of errors that would determine a passing or failing score.

<u>Failing portfolios</u> do not include all of the required materials and/or do not as a whole exhibit a basic mastery of the goals of ENGL 1033 and usually exhibit the characteristics detailed below. Overall, the selections in a failing portfolio show that the student cannot adequately narrow a topic—either all of the essays are too broad or one of the essays is egregiously broad—or that the student consistently gets off topic. Often, more than one essay lacks a clear, arguable thesis or main point but instead may contain a statement of fact, an announcement of intent, or other sentence masquerading as a thesis. Student often fails to make appropriate rhetorical choices (tone, point of view, genre, etc) for the discourse community being addressed. Introductions, in fact, may reveal that the student has not considered the audience or purpose of the piece because the topic has not been justified or contextualized. A majority of the essays merely summarize primary sources or repeat secondary sources without much critical thought that would apply, extend, or critique those positions. Paragraphs in general may be inconsistent with thesis as well as underdeveloped. Even if the points are somewhat interesting, evidence may be missing from paragraphs or be overly general. Usually, failing portfolios do not demonstrate much consistent organization, and thus points may not be arranged in any clear or logical order. Telltale signs of this lack of organization are disunity in paragraph content and the absence of transitional phrases, repetition, or synonyms. Quotes and paraphrases, if present, are not usually introduced or tied back to thesis and may even lack proper citation

bordering on unintentional plagiarism. Interpretations of textual evidence are sometimes highly inaccurate or unfair and demonstrate that the student has not grasped either the source material or the concepts she or he is applying to it. On the sentence level, the portfolio may contain traces of style and voice, but those efforts are inconsistent and sometimes inappropriate. Errors in conventions of grammar and mechanics (particularly major errors like fragments, subject-verb agreement, comma splices, run-ons, dangling modifiers, and pronoun reference) consistently distract readers from the content of the portfolio.

Mid-Term Portfolio Results
You will receive the results of your portfolio evaluation from your instructor shortly after the mid-term portfolio review.

UNIVERSITY OF TULSA WRITING PROGRAM

INSTRUCTIONS FOR COMPILING YOUR FINAL ENGL 1033 WRITING PORTFOLIO

Use these general guidelines as you prepare your writing portfolio for your ENGL 1033 class. Although this handout is designed to help you through the process of compiling the portfolio, feel free to ask your instructor for more detailed explanations on any aspect of the process.

Ongoing Student File

Throughout the semester, you should keep a file of your own in which you preserve *all* of the work that you produce in class. The file should include drafts of papers you have written as well as revised papers that have been returned to you. You might even want to include class notes, memos that you have written to your instructor, and other relevant items. Keep the file in a safe place where you will not lose it because you will choose the contents of your 1033 writing portfolio from the file at midterm and then again near the end of the semester. *Keep in mind that you will not get your final portfolio back as it will serve as a record of your achievement in this course.* Make photocopies of any papers you would like to keep.

Final Portfolio Due Date

Please consult your course syllabus for the final portfolio due date. **Please note: NO LATE PORTFOLIOS WILL BE ACCEPTED.**

Final Portfolio Contents

Your portfolio, which will be evaluated on a pass/fail basis, should include an introductory reflective essay written according to the directions below, one of your unrevised in-class essays, and two revised essays. One of the revised essays must include at least a short essay using the textbook as a source and a longer essay using at least three academic sources.

Remember that you have a better chance of passing the portfolio evaluation if you revise these papers further—perhaps even *several* times during the semester—using your instructor and the Writing Center as resources during the process. When you compile your portfolio, make sure to include *all* of the following items because incomplete portfolios do not pass:

Final Portfolio Contents Checklist
❑ Introductory reflective essay (2-3 pages)   ❑ One unrevised in-class essay   ❑ One revised 3- to 4-page paper (with the course textbook as a source)   ❑ One revised 5- to 6-page paper (using at least 3 academic sources in addition to the primary text)

Academic Sources

Academic sources are defined by the Writing Program as peer-reviewed articles or books from a particular discipline or discourse community (see section "The Research Process" for more information). Regardless of whether they come from print or electronic resources, these books and articles typically have extensive bibliographies and/or footnoted sources. Acceptable academic sources include journals like the *James Joyce Quarterly* or *Tulsa Studies in Women's Literature* and books like Lars Engle's *Shakespearean Pragmatism* or Holly Laird's *Women Coauthors* (See the "The Process of Research" section of this Guide for more details on what counts as an academic source). Keep in mind that many web pages that you may find through Google or another internet search engine are most likely not academic (See the Library Resource section of this

Guide for more information on finding and using adequate electronic resources). Not having the required number of academic sources is grounds for portfolio failure.

Introductory Reflective Essay

The introductory reflective essay will be placed first in your portfolio and will be among the most important papers that you write all semester. Besides introducing the other papers in the portfolio, your introductory essay presents an argument to convince the Portfolio Committee that your portfolio meets the requirements and objectives of the course. Your introductory essay will also demonstrate your ability to think critically about the strengths and weaknesses of your own writing process and to recognize the particular features and patterns that emerge as you create a product presented to a particular audience. Remember that first impressions are important, and the essay will be the first piece of your writing that portfolio readers see. As Nedra Reynolds writes in *Portfolio Keeping*, portfolio readers will be looking for "writers who are insightful, conscientious, and engaged in learning" (45). Your essays should have clear organizational structures, each including an introduction, a body (in which you provide supporting evidence of your claims about your work), and a conclusion that leads readers into the rest of your portfolio. Your reflective essay *must include all* of the following elements:

- ❑ Paragraph structure with thesis, body, and conclusion
- ❑ Discussion of each item chosen for inclusion in the portfolio
- ❑ Thoughtful reflection about your writing process
- ❑ Assessment of the strengths and weaknesses of your own work
- ❑ Concrete examples from your own writing for support

You will probably want to use *some* of the following suggestions adapted from *Portfolio Keeping*, but remember that you are *not* expected to use all of them:

- Do not merely summarize your papers—the reviewers will be reading them—but instead draw on them for evidence to support your points about what you have learned and what you still need to work on.
- Discuss which paper you consider your best one and explain why.
- Explain in detail the revisions that you have made to one or more of the pieces, pointing out particular improvements that you want readers to notice.
- Indicate the particular strengths of each item in the portfolio.
- Take the reader through the process that you followed in writing one or more of the papers.
- Explain what your portfolio as a whole demonstrates about you as a writer, student, researcher, or critical thinker.
- Acknowledge your weaknesses as a writer but show how you have worked—and are continuing to work—to overcome them.
- Acknowledge how responses from your classmates and instructor have influenced the writing included in your portfolio.
- Reflect on what you have learned about writing through reading, writing, and discussion.
- Identify particular features or patterns of your writing process.
- Indicate which writing strategies worked well for you and which worked less well, explaining why you believe this to be the case.
- Discuss which piece of writing you enjoyed most or least and explain why.

(Reynolds 44)

Your introductory reflective essay should be between two and three typed pages long.

Preparing Your Portfolio

Submit your portfolio to your instructor in the official portfolio folder that came with this guide. Replacements for lost folders are available in the university bookstore in ACAC. Once you have obtained a folder, insert the required materials in the right order. The introductory reflective essay should be first, but you should organize the other papers strategically to showcase your writing ability. If portfolio readers read your best essay last, for example, they may feel more positively about your portfolio as a whole than they would if they read a less successful paper last.

Remove your name and your instructor's name from each of the papers you include in your portfolio, otherwise you may fail review. Instead of your name, include your **complete TU student ID number** along with the course number *and* section number on each page of each essay and on the outside of the portfolio folder.

Final Portfolio Preparation Checklist

- ❑ Use official portfolio folder
- ❑ Remove student and instructor names
- ❑ Place ID number on all papers and on folder
- ❑ Include course number *and* section number on all papers and on folder
- ❑ Place introductory essay first
- ❑ Include all required items (See above check list)
- ❑ Make sure all essays meet minimum page and source number requirements

Final Portfolio Scoring Criteria

Your portfolio will be scored by a committee of reviewers from the Writing Program according to the following criteria. The following chart closely resembles the scoring sheet that committee reviewers will be using to assess your work.

Final Portfolio Scoring Sheet

Course Section Number: _____   Student ID Number: _____   Reviewer Number: _____

A passing portfolio should demonstrate that the student has a basic mastery of the objectives of ENGL 1033 and should meet the following criteria. Reviewers may evaluate each portfolio holistically or analytically, weighing its components equally.

If a portfolio does not contain one of the following elements below, please check "Retake" at the bottom of this sheet.

Yes	No	
☐	☐	Introductory essay
☐	☐	In-class essay
☐	☐	One essay with at least three full pages and a class reading source in Works Cited
☐	☐	One longer essay with a least five full pages and three academic sources plus a class reading in Works Cited
☐	☐	Works Cited pages for previous two essays

After a thorough reading of student work, please check the following elements as they apply. Portfolio exhibits:

☐	☐	Arguments generally unified around a central idea or thesis
☐	☐	Topics adequately narrow for length of essays
☐	☐	Overall content that demonstrates critical thinking (apply, extend, critique)
☐	☐	Appropriate rhetorical choices considering audience, purpose, tone, and point of view
☐	☐	Introductions that attempt to justify and contextualize thesis within a discourse community; conclusions that connect argument to larger concerns of that community
☐	☐	Development and organization of points logically and coherently
☐	☐	Adequate use of detail and evidence to support points
☐	☐	Effective integration and responsible MLA documentation of required no. of textual sources
☐	☐	Attempts to convey style and voice (diction, figures of speech, syntax, sentence variety, etc)
☐	☐	Awareness of conventions of Standard American English so that errors do not obscure content

---

Please include any written comments on the reverse of this form. Check recommendation for portfolio score below:

Pass	Retake	
☐	☐	Portfolio Score. "Retake" indicates that students do not meet standards and must retake the course.

PORTFOLIOS THAT CONTAIN PAPERS THAT DO NOT MEET THE MINIMUM PAGE RE-QUIREMENTS WILL FAIL. So please make sure that all papers meet the requirements.

The following rubric gives a general, or holistic, description of the qualities of passing and failing portfolios. Reviewers will decide which category best fits with a particular portfolio in deciding results. This rubric supplements the analytical rubric (above) that divides portfolio assessment into it elements, each one reflecting an objective of the course as stated in the syllabus.

A <u>passing portfolio</u> should demonstrate that the student has a basic mastery of the objectives of ENGL 1033 and should fit this profile in most aspects. As a whole, the passing portfolio shows that the student can narrow a topic adequately for the given length of an essay and that he or she can stay on topic with only a few minor digressions. The contents of the portfolio also reveal that the student has made rhetorical choices (tone, point of view, genre, etc.) appropriate to the audience and purpose of the piece (both of which should be apparently implied in the argument). Introductions attempt to justify why the argument is necessary for a particular discourse community and place the thesis in a relevant context, even if the student may not completely understand that community. Overall, the content of the portfolio makes attempts at critical thinking, whether that be application, extension, or critique (aka "reading against the grain") of a text or discourse community. Concerning paragraphs, all major points are unified with the central idea or thesis and are supported with adequate, concrete textual evidence. Evidence is often but not always related back to the thesis coherently (transitions, repetition, synonyms, etc.) and is organized and developed in a consistent and sustained, if sometimes sloppy, manner (using modes of development—definition, cause/effect, proposal, illustration, etc.; with a logical order—chronological, emphatic, spatial, etc.). Pieces of writing usually integrate textual sources fairly, accurately, and effectively with only some formal mistakes or potential misreadings. Portfolio should not fail for misreadings alone. Citation style may not be completely accurate but should demonstrate an attempt to credit sources when necessary to avoid plagiarism. Conclusion may summarize main points but should also attempt to spell out ramifications of the argument for a particular discourse community. On the sentence level, the portfolio should reveal attempts to convey style and voice through diction, syntax, figurative language, etc. on at least a minimal level. Passing portfolios also exhibit control of conventions of Standard American English so that errors do not overly inhibit content of argument. There is no set limit of errors that would determine a passing or failing score.

<u>Failing portfolios</u> do not include all of the required materials and/or do not as a whole exhibit a basic mastery of the goals of ENGL 1033 and usually exhibit the characteristics detailed below. Overall, the selections in a failing portfolio show that the student cannot adequately narrow a topic—either all of the essays are too broad or one of the essays is egregiously broad—or that the student consistently gets off topic. Often, more than one essay lacks a clear, arguable thesis or main point but instead may contain a statement of fact, an announcement of intent, or other sentence masquerading as a thesis. Student often fails to make appropriate rhetorical choices (tone, point of view, genre, etc) for the discourse community being addressed. Introductions, in fact, may reveal that the student has not considered the audience or purpose of the piece because the topic has not been justified or contextualized. A majority of the essays merely summarize primary sources or repeat secondary sources without much critical thought that would apply, extend, or critique those positions. Paragraphs in general may be inconsistent with thesis as well as underdeveloped. Even if the points are somewhat interesting, evidence may be missing from paragraphs or be overly general. Usually, failing portfolios do not demonstrate much consistent organization, and thus points may not be arranged in any clear or logical order. Telltale signs of this lack of organization are disunity in paragraph content and the absence of transitional phrases, repetition, or synonyms. Quotes and paraphrases, if present, are not usually introduced or tied back to thesis and may even lack proper citation bordering on unintentional plagiarism. Interpretations of textual evidence are sometimes highly inaccurate or unfair and demonstrate that the student has not grasped either the source material or the concepts she

or he is applying to it. On the sentence level, the portfolio may contain traces of style and voice, but those efforts are inconsistent and sometimes inappropriate. Errors in conventions of grammar and mechanics (particularly major errors like fragments, subject-verb agreement, comma splices, run-ons, dangling modifiers, and pronoun reference) consistently distract readers from the content of the portfolio.

Final Portfolio Results
You will receive the results of your portfolio evaluation from your instructor before the end of the term.

CAMPUS WRITING RESOURCES

GENERAL INFORMATION

The following resources will help you successfully complete your writing requirements here at the university. These resources are not just for students in the Writing Program either; you can take advantage of most of them throughout your entire career in school.

Faculty Office Hours

Instructors at the University of Tulsa keep regular office hours for the convenience of their students. These times are listed on course syllabi as well as in the English Department office. Office hours are designed to help you in many ways. Coming in during office hours allows you to receive one-on-one help with your instructor about any questions or concerns you might have. These issues may include your progress and personal learning in the course. Students often feel like they should only come in during office hours when they are struggling with an assignment. In truth, office hours are a great way for you to get regular, personal help or clarification concerning specific questions that you might have about the course. While email is also a viable alternative for contacting instructors, office hours often provide the opportunity for quick and interactive feedback and discussion. Generally speaking, graduating students often express the wish that they had taken better advantage of their instructors' office hours. In the case that your particular schedule does not permit you to come by during regularly scheduled office hours, most instructors are very amenable to setting up a specific appointment that works with the needs of the individual student. Please do not hesitate to expand your education through increased faculty interaction via office hours.

The Writing Center

The University of Tulsa offers the benefit of a well-staffed Writing Center that provides assistance at no cost for all students at every level of the writing process. The Writing Center is operated by the Writing Program and is run by highly qualified English graduate students with years of writing experience behind them. The Writing Center, currently located on the first floor of Chapman Hall next to the Lecture Hall, offers writing consultations on all ranges of student papers. If you are having trouble understanding an assignment, learning how to put a comma in the right place, drafting, outlining, or even putting the finishing touches on your works cited page, the Writing Center can help.

To the dismay of some, the Writing Center is not an editing service. However, what it can provide for a student is professional assistance in learning to find your mistakes, fix your mistakes, and integrating advanced skills and techniques in all of your college-level writing. While the Writing Center cannot guarantee an "A" on any assignment, it can ensure that at the end of our intensive consultation you will walk away having learned or improved upon skills to become a better writer. The sessions typically last a minimum of a half an hour so that the consultant has enough time to work with your particular questions and needs and so that you walk away knowing that you have learned something and not that your work has been done for you.

On top of the invaluable consulting services provided by the Writing Center, computers are available for you to work in a relaxed and quiet study atmosphere. If you need someplace to work on your papers in between classes you are welcome to come in and use one of our computers. We also have a printer at your disposal. Please remember:

o The Writing Center is a free service provided by the University for the use of students at any level. You do not have to be a Writing Program Student to schedule a consultation. Remember this when you get into your upper-level major courses that require you to write.

o While we try to assist all students to the best of our abilities, the Writing Center is a heavily used service. It is always best to make an appointment well in advance of your paper's due date in order to ensure an effective session with enough time to implement suggestions.

o If you are going to be late or unable to make your appointment, please let us know as far in advance as possible. If you are more than 15 minutes late, we may give your time slot to another student.

o Please bring with you to the consultation the writing assignment, two copies of your paper, the textbook, any relevant materials used in the paper, and your student ID.

Writing Center
Phone Number: 631-3131
Email: writingcenter@utulsa.edu
Hours: <http://www.cas.utulsa.edu/english/writingcenter/>

The Writing Center is free for the use of all students at TU. Do not hesitate to schedule an appointment at the telephone number or email above.

Center for Student Academic Support (CSAS)

The Center for Student Academic Support (CSAS) is a valuable resource for writing students. The Center provides various programs and services in an attempt to help your meet your academic goals. The CSAS website identifies the following as services provided by the Center:

- Academic skills workshops such as test preparation, study strategies, note taking, effective interaction with faculty, and many other programs.
- Identification and monitoring of students at risk.
- Initial referral to other campus support services.
- Liaison between students and faculty or other university personnel.
- Tutoring and tutor training.
- Consultation on an individual basis.
- Screening, evaluation, and assessment of student interests, skills, and abilities.
- Accommodations for student with disabilities.

Services offered by CSAS are generally free, though tutoring sessions for introductory courses cost $5 per hour (a bargain price for tutoring). Many of their services (workshops, etc.) will be advertised on campus, and the CSAS website <http://www.utulsa.edu/academicsupport> includes a listing of their scheduled programs and activities.

The Center for Student Academic Support
Lorton Hall, Room 210
Hours: Monday-Friday 8 a.m.-5 p.m.
631-2315
<http://www.utulsa.edu/academicsupport>

If you have any special needs or disabilities, contact the Center for Student Academic Support and they will assist you in securing the appropriate accommodations in compliance with the Americans with Disabilities Act.

Computer Use

In your writing courses, you are expected to use computers for a variety of tasks such as writing papers, using word processing software such as Microsoft Word, and doing research through the McFarlin Library online catalogue. All University of Tulsa students have free access to computers and printers in the campus computer labs (see "Campus Computer Labs" section regarding location and availability of labs). Students are encouraged to make use of personal disk space on the TU filer (W drive), a system which allows you to save and retrieve your documents from the campus server. See the section on "Using Filer" for additional information.

To save documents using the campus version of Microsoft Word, either use the "File" pull down menu (located at the top left of your computer screen) to "save as," thus making sure you direct your file to the appropriate "save as" location (e.g.: W drive/filer, or desktop.) Remember, if you save to desktop files will be "wiped" from the system every 24 hours. Save to your W drive "filer" location or removable flash drive to ensure availability of your file. A shortcut may also be used to save your file. Press "control + S," and make sure of the location where you file will be saved. Control + S will also allow you to do a "quick save." Again, using the filer or a removable flash drive will ensure the future availability of your file.

With the newer versions of Microsoft Word you will need to save your file in the "compatibility mode," so that your file can be used with older versions of Microsoft Word, as well as with the newer version. If you use the newer version and do not save in the compatibility mode, you will not be able to open your file with the older versions of Word. In the later versions of Word, to the left of the "HOME" tab, is a multi-colored icon. Click this icon and you will now see a listing of various choices. Choose and click "Save As." Then direct your pointer to the right of your selection where the "Word 97 – 2003" option is located in order to save your document in the compatibility mode. Make sure your file is saved to a location where you may retrieve it easily.

26

Campus Computer Labs

Computers for writing are available in several locations around campus. McFarlin Library houses the Pauline Walter Academic Technology Center which has two computer labs (called "iLabs") that are available for student use. In addition, the Writing Center has several machines for use during its regular hours (see "Writing Center" above in this section). Access to other labs on campus various by class, college or major. Please check with the Dean's office for availability.

> For the most current information on lab equipment and hours, please contact the Help Desk (below) or check the Information Services website <http://www.is.utulsa.edu/facilities/labs/>.

Labs are monitored by student workers who are trained to maintain the printers and assist you with basic computer use and operation. These workers are not necessarily computer experts but can assist with simple operations such as refilling the printer paper, changing the toner cartridge, etc. Please do not expect them to help you recover lost or corrupted files or to provide assistance with your writing assignments. If you have hardware, software, or network problems, please call the Help Desk (see below). Unfortunately, the Help Desk cannot help you with your personal computer.

> **The Help Desk**
> McFarlin Library, Room 1085
> 631.3500
> help@utulsa.edu

Using "Filer"

Each student is allowed 3GB of space for personal use on a campus server, lovingly referred to as the "filer." You can access your space through filer, which requires your TU user-name and password, and no one else can get into your space without that information. This space is accessible from computers both on and off campus and is backed-up by TU nightly. Should there be a problem with your computer or with the server, your information is recoverable.

To use filer on a campus computer, you may either click on the 'Utulsa Home' icon on the desktop, or if you are saving a document you currently have open, chose 'W:' as the location (the 'W:' may be accompanied by 'filer space' or '(your user-name) on filer'). For instructions on how to access filer from an off-campus computer, visit <http://www.is.utulsa.edu/services/uhome>.

Disks are an outdated, unstable method of saving your information; even a cell phone ringing nearby can corrupt your disk. In most cases, the Help Desk is unable to recover documents from corrupted disks. To save your work, you should use a more stable form of portable memory, such as a jump or flash drive, or use filer. Since filer is a free service offered to all students that is backed-up and recoverable by the University, many teachers will not accept corrupted computer files as an excuse for late work.

Vista

Another computer resource that you may encounter in your writing class, along with many of your other classes, is Vista (also referred to as "Blackboard" or "WebCT [Web Course Tools]"). Vista is a web-based interface that moves classroom interactions and learning beyond the classroom. The Vista interface is used by instructors throughout the university as a means of on-line interaction and communication with students. Most instructors in the Writing Program do use Vista, though the extent to which they use the program varies greatly. Some instructors may use only the communication (e-mail or discussion) functions whereas other instructors may post assignments and other materials online. Similarly, some instructors may require you to participate in on-line discussions or submit homework or assignments via Vista. Instructors who chose to do so may even post grades via Vista.

Even though your writing instructor may not require you to use Vista within his/her course, you will probably be required to use Vista (or perhaps a similar interface) at some time during your academic career. The guidelines and instructions that follow are by no mean exhaustive; they are simply here to help you become more familiar with the basics of TU's Vista interface.

Logging On to Vista. The following instructions will allow you to access Vista on or off campus:
1. Go to <https://webct.utulsa.edu/>.
2. Click on "My Courses"
3. After Vista runs a "Browser Check" (and you have made any necessary updates), click on "Vista Courses"
4. In the "Log in" box, enter your TU username and password and connect to the system (this is the same one you uses to log on to a computer and to check email).
5. To enter the site for a specific class, simply click on the title of the course in your "Course List."

If you need assistance with Vista, you may go to <http://www.is.utulsa.edu/services/webct/> or use the "Help" tool which can be found at the top of any Vista page. If you are having problems logging on to the university computer system, contact the Computer Help Desk. If you need help with you password or need to have it reset, you must go to the Help Desk with your student id. (See "Computer Lab" section for Help Desk info)

Turnitin.com

Some writing instructors may require students to electronically upload their papers to a website called "turnitin.com." This website checks your paper against a vast database of other student papers, professional magazines and journals, and pages across the Web. The purpose of this website is to remind students that plagiarism is not tolerated at The University of Tulsa (see "Writing Program Policies" section for the TU Plagiarism Statement) and that doing your own work is the best way to learn. Turnitin.com also ultimately protects the integrity and originality of your work from unauthorized use by others. If required to use it, please ask your instructor for directions on uploading your essay files to this site through Vista.

WRITING PROGRAM POLICIES

Although writing courses at The University of Tulsa vary in topic, readings, and approach, there are several policies that apply to all courses in the Writing Program. Those program-wide requirements are elaborated below. Keep in mind that these policies often represent *minimum* requirements—your instructor may have a more stringent, say, absence policy than is required by the Program. Please consult your writing course syllabus or speak to your instructor regarding any details you do not understand.

Attendance Policy

Students must be made aware of the attendance policy that governs courses in the University Writing Program. Statements of the Writing Program policy, requirements, and student responsibilities are furnished on the syllabus.

The University of Tulsa honors a freedom of attendance policy, which states that the "student should be free to attend class or not to attend class in those classes where fair academic evaluation does not necessitate direct student participation." However, Writing Program courses qualify as exceptions. Therefore, the Writing Program has an official attendance policy. Please note that this policy concerns unexcused absences. We do not penalize students for absences for which the student has an official university excuse.

Although your instructor may have more stringent penalties for unexcused absences, the Program sets minimum consequences. Unexcused absences for 10 percent of the scheduled class meetings constitute grounds for lowering your final grade by one letter grade; unexcused absences for 15 percent of the scheduled class meetings constitute grounds for lowering the final grade by two letters; unexcused absences for 20 percent of the scheduled class meetings are grounds for failure. The chart below summarizes the penalties:

```
For a MWF class:
    10 percent is 4 absences – loss of one letter grade
    15 percent is 6 absences – loss of two letter grades
    20 percent is 8 absences – grounds for an F
```

```
For a TTH class:
    10 percent is 3 absences – loss of one letter grade
    15 percent is 4 absences – loss of two letter grades
    20 percent is 6 absences – grounds for an F
```

ENGL 1004 also requires students to attend at least six out of eight weeks of workshops. Missing more than two weeks of workshops is grounds for an F. Remember that it is a four credit course and that you must attend workshops in order to attain that full credit.

In part, this policy is discretionary. The instructor decides what constitutes missing class and whether the absence is excused or unexcused. However, enforcement of the policy where the grounds exist is not discretionary. Instructors are obligated to follow the above policy, and you should be made aware of that fact.

The attendance policy is not difficult to meet when you consider that you only meet with your class 3 or 4 hours per week. Several times during the semester your instructor may choose to inform you of your absences and your situation regarding a potential drop in letter grade. But you are ultimately responsible for making it to class and knowing your instructor's attendance policy.

This policy carries with it two implications:

First, students who enroll late will already have accrued absences, even though the university allows students to add courses at virtually any time, as long as the faculty member for the class permits it. In the Writing Program, we do not generally allow students to enroll after the first week of classes, except in extraordinary circumstances. Students who wish to enroll past what the instructor feels is an appropriate time must see the Director of the Writing Program.

Second, students must verify their absences from class. Let your instructor know that you will be out of class before you miss class, if possible. You may call his or her office and leave a message, send an email message, or drop a note in the mailbox in the English department. Students who miss class for any reason must give a written note upon their return to class if they want the absence to be excused. If your instructor does not receive a note from you, they will consider the absence unexcused.

Sometimes major illness, heavy extra-curricular requirements, or other life problems cause a student to miss several class sessions. However, every missed class session potentially compromises your ability to do the work of a writing course. Your instructor may confer with you if your total absences approach the 10 percent mark.

Student-Teacher Conferences

Student-teacher conferences are a vital part of TU's Writing Program, and students are required in ENGL 1004 and 1033 to meet at least twice with their instructors. Studies indicate that students benefit greatly from personal, one-on-one feedback and interaction. As a result, your instructor will schedule times for you to come in for one-on-one conferencing. These conferences are a time for you to receive individualized help with your writing. Although your instructor cannot possibly provide you with all-inclusive feedback in each conference (writing is a process rather than a one-stop visit), these conferences will be very useful in helping you recognize your individual strengths and weaknesses. Conferences are considered to be so important that regular classroom instruction is sometimes cancelled during conference times.

Tips for Conferencing:
1) **Be punctual**. Arriving late can push things off schedule and limit the attention other students receive (or cut your own session short!)

2) **Be as prepared as possible**. Read over any feedback you have received on the current essay you're working on and jot down a list of questions you want to ask. Don't simply rely on your memory. The readier you are for your conference, the more you will learn from your instructor during your conference time.

3) **Be proactive**. Students who expect to be told what to grammatically "fix" often leave conferences somewhat disappointed. Instructors are not going to edit your papers. Expect open feedback from your instructor on how you can improve, and look for ways to apply the help that you are given. Taking responsibility for your own writing is vital to good conferencing.

4) **Be open-minded**. Remember that feedback from your instructor is important! Students occasionally take conference feedback to mean they are doing something wrong, when in fact the converse is true. The things your instructor will share with you are designed to improve your writing, so stay positive in your conference. An instructor who says a lot of things to you obviously feels like there are a lot of good things happening in your paper!

5) **Take notes**. It is difficult to remember everything your instructor tells you, and students who do not take notes inevitably struggle to remember the helpful instruction they have received in their conference.

You are responsible for remembering and being on time to your conference. Some instructors, especially the ones who call class during conference weeks, may count you absent for an entire week of classes, which in a MWF section would add up to three unexcused absences. See the "Absence Policy" section for more information.

Late Work and Failure to Turn in Work

In order to pass any writing course, you must turn in all assigned work. There are no exceptions. If you miss an in-class assignment that counts toward your grade, that assignment must be made up. Even if the assignment does not count toward the grade, you should expect to make it up. Instructors are not likely to make deals with students who have fallen behind due to their own negligence. If your instructor requires a rough draft of a paper, turn in a rough draft, as well as the final paper.

Late work is a perennial problem, and you should recognize that students who fall behind are likely to fail. Most instructors clearly state their late work policies right in their syllabus, but the details of the policy may vary from instructor to instructor. Some instructors allow students to turn in one paper late without penalty, if it is turned in on the next working day. Other instructors deduct a percentage of the grade, say 10%, for each day or class period the paper is late. *Even if the point value of the paper whittles to zero, you must turn in the paper to pass the course.*

Policy Regarding "Incomplete" Grades

The Writing Program policy is that we do not give incompletes as final grades. Because of the nature of our courses, it is hard for students to finish their work without the benefit of classroom discussion, tutorials, and instructor conferences. Our experience tells us that students rarely finish the work; they fall behind in their courses of study; the incomplete changes to an F after a year; and the students are worse off than they would have been if they had dropped the course and started over. The general rule is that you must have attended at least 80% of the classes to qualify for an incomplete. If your instructor believes that you have a legitimate reason to take an incomplete, he or she will notify the Writing Program Director to discuss what procedure will work best for you.

Plagiarism

Because plagiarism is such an important issue in any writing course, we have devoted an entire section to our policy regarding it. The next few pages of this guide are perhaps the most important you will read for your writing course. In fact, you will be required to sign a form (which may be found in the Appendix) acknowledging that you fully understand and will abide by The University of Tulsa Writing Program Plagiarism policy.

THE UNIVERSITY WRITING PROGRAM

PLAGIARISM STATEMENT

The following statement defines and describes plagiarism, gives general guidelines and examples for using sources in essays, and sets the policies on plagiarism for courses in the University Writing Program. This statement has been endorsed by the College of Arts and Sciences of The University of Tulsa. Although policies on plagiarism may vary among courses and definitions of plagiarism may be extended in some fields, this statement offers guidelines and policies on plagiarism that are generally accepted in the liberal arts. Students in Writing Program courses will be asked to read and discuss this statement and sign a statement confirming that they understand it.

Plagiarism Defined

Plagiarism is claiming someone else's work as your own. Ideas circulate freely in an intellectual community, and intellectual inquiry often depends on use of ideas borrowed from others. Responsible writers, however, indicate their debts to others by clearly citing borrowed material. Plagiarism occurs when writers fail to cite their borrowings. Auto-plagiarism consists in plagiarizing yourself. In the context of your coursework as a student, auto-plagiarism would occur if you resubmitted any of your own work—whether a complete assignment or only part of it—as if it were freshly submitted.

Plagiarized work is easy to recognize because it does not clearly indicate borrowing. It is full of facts, observations, and ideas the writer could not have developed on his or her own and is written in a style different from that of the writer. By clearly indicating your debts to other writers, you can both avoid plagiarism and call attention to your own original ideas.

Integrating Sources

Understanding the different ways you can incorporate source material into your writing is crucial to avoiding plagiarism:

Quotation ("quote" for short): a word-for-word copy of someone else's words. Indicate a quoted passage by enclosing it in quotation marks ("") or, if it is longer than four lines, by setting it apart from the main text in an indented block. The source of the quotation must also be cited, either in the text or in a footnote or endnote.

Paraphrase: a restatement in your own words of something your source has said. One purpose of paraphrasing, as opposed to quoting, is to put something into words your audience will understand. For example, articles in popular science magazines often paraphrase more difficult articles in science journals. Putting something into your own words is an important intellectual activity in its own right: it shows that you understand and can work with the material. Putting an idea in your own words does not make it yours. Although neither quotation marks nor block indention are needed, a paraphrase must be cited.

Summary: resembles a paraphrase but is much shorter and follows the sources less closely than a paraphrase does. You must cite the source that you are summarizing.

Citation: identifies the source of a quotation, paraphrase or summary. Citation practices vary considerably in different types of writing, but most academic and professional writing requires a full citation in the text, in a combination of brief parenthetical citations in the text and complete bibliographic entries in a list of Works Cited, or in footnotes or endnotes.

Types of Plagiarism

1. **Direct Plagiarism:** This is copying a source word for word without indicating that it is a quotation and crediting the author.

2. **Borrowing work from other students:** There is nothing wrong with students helping each other or sharing information, but you must write your own essays. This includes having another student dictate to you as you write their words down. Turning in a paper that someone else has written is an especially severe case of direct plagiarism.

3. **Vague or Incorrect Citation:** A writer should clearly indicate where borrowing begins and ends because not to do so, though it seems innocent, is plagiarism. *This is why it is so important to learn a citation style such as MLA style* (see next section for more information). Sometimes, a writer cites a source once, and the reader assumes that the previous sentence or paragraph has been paraphrased, when most of the essay is a paraphrase of this one source. The writer has failed to indicate his borrowings clearly. Paraphrases and summaries should be indicated as such by surrounding them with citation——at the beginning with the author's name, at the end with a parenthetical reference. The writer must always clearly indicate when a paraphrase, summary, or quotation begins, ends, or is interrupted.

4. **Auto-plagiarism:** This happens when an author plagiarizes his or her own writing. Students' best work usually occurs through revisions of previous drafts. But auto-plagiarism takes place when a student presents any prior writing, usually from another course or school, as entirely fresh work for course credit. A previous assignment—whether in whole or part—may **not** be offered as if it were a fresh submission to a course instructor.

5. **Mosaic Plagiarism:** This is the most common type of plagiarism. The writer does not copy the source directly, but changes a few words in each sentence or slightly reworks a paragraph, without giving credit to the original author. Those sentences or paragraphs are not quotations, but they are so close to quotation that they should be quoted directly or, if they have been changed enough to qualify as a paraphrase, the source should be cited.

Penalties for Plagiarism

No plagiarized paper will be accepted for credit in any Writing Program course at the University of Tulsa. This includes partially plagiarized papers. A plagiarized paper will automatically receive an "F" grade. If the instructor feels that the plagiarism was unintentional, he or she may ask the student to rewrite the paper for credit. By reading this plagiarism handout and by affirming that you understand plagiarism, however, you assume responsibility for any plagiarism that occurs in your essays.

Plagiarism may be grounds for failure in a Writing Program course. Even if a student's course grades average out to a passing grade when the "F" from a plagiarized paper is counted in, the instructor may still give the student an "F" for the course.

Instructors who suspect that a student has plagiarized will submit a letter explaining the reasons for their suspicions and a copy of the student's paper to the Director of the Writing Program, who will keep them on file. All cases of suspected plagiarism that occur in Writing Program courses will be reviewed by the Director of the Writing Program. Any student who is suspected of plagiarism will have the opportunity to discuss the matter with the Director of the Writing Program.

At the end of each academic term, the Director of the Writing Program submits a list of plagiarizers to each college dean. Repeat offenders may be dismissed from the University.

Why Students Plagiarize

Some students are tempted to paraphrase because they find writing college-level essays difficult or intimidating. Such students sometimes become frustrated when an essay on which they have worked long and hard is returned with many corrections and a low grade. Frustrated and afraid of failure, they may resort to copying an essay word for word or making only a few slight changes in the wording.

Rather than plagiarizing, these students should seek assistance from their instructor, from the Writing Center, from a special tutor, from the Center for Student Academic Support, or from the Counseling Center, which can provide assistance in dealing not only with a learning disability, but also with frustration, fear, and stress. The Writing Program offers intensive consultations in avoiding plagiarism. For information, see the "Writing Center" section in this guide or call the Writing Center directly (631-3131).

Other students write well enough but find plagiarism tempting because they fear earning a grade lower than they or their parents expect, have fallen behind in their coursework and feel that they lack the time to write a competent essay, or feel that they cannot handle the assigned task or generate good ideas on the subject.

Start writing, even if the writing begins as a summary of some other piece of writing, and you will usually discover that you have something to say. If you fall behind, talk with your instructor. He or she may penalize you for submitting work late, but late work is preferable to plagiarized work. If you feel overwhelmed by your course work and unable to keep up, arrange to visit a counselor at the Counseling Center. He or she can help you learn to manage your time and the stress of university life better.

Plagiarizing an essay is never an acceptable solution.

A Case of Plagiarism

Richard Marius, in his statement on plagiarism for Harvard University, cites a case of mosaic plagiarism. G. R. V. Barratt, in the introduction to *The Decembrist Memoirs*, plagiarized from several works, including *The Decembrists* by Marc Raeff. In one passage, Raeff had written:

> December 14, 1825, was the day set for taking the oath of allegiance to the new Emperor, Nicholas I. Only a few days earlier, on November 27, when news of the death of Alexander I had reached the capital, an oath of allegiance had been taken to Nicholas's older brother, Grand Duke Constantine, Viceroy of Poland. But in accordance with the act of renunciation he had made in 1819, Constantine had refused the crown. The virtual interregnum stirred society and produced uneasiness among the troops, and the government was apprehensive of disorders and disturbances. Police agents reported the existence of secret societies and rumors of a coup to be staged by regiments of the Guards. The new Emperor was anxious to have the oath taken as quickly and quietly as possible. The members of the central government institutions—Council of State, Senate, Ministries—took the oath without incident, early in the morning. In most regiments of the garrison the oath was also taken peaceably.

Barratt presented the same paragraph with only a few words and details changed:

> December 14, 1825, was the day on which the Guards' regiments in Petersburg were to swear solemn allegiance to Nicholas I, the new Emperor. Less than three weeks before, when news of the death of Alexander I had reached the capital from Taganrog on the sea of Azov, an oath, no less solemn and binding, had been taken to Nicholas's elder brother, the Grand Duke Constantine, viceroy of Poland. Constantine, however, had declined to be emperor, in accordance with two separate acts of renunciation made in 1819 and, secretly, in 1822. The effective interregnum caused uneasiness both in society and in the army. The government feared undefined disorders—with some reason, since police agents reported the existence of various clandestine groups and rumours of a coup to be effected by guardsmen. Nicholas was anxious that the oath be sworn to him promptly and quietly. At first it would seem that he would have his way; senators, ministers, and members of the Council of State took the oath by 9 A. M. In most regiments of the garrison the oath was also taken peaceably.

To see why this is mosaic plagiarism, compare these two versions line by line. What changes has Barratt made? Why do you think he made these changes? Why is this a case of plagiarism even though Barratt has made changes?

Guidelines for Proper Use of Sources

1. Enclose direct quotations in quotation marks. If the quotation is longer than four lines, indent it in block format. In both cases, cite the source by using MLA in-text parenthetical style and by entering the source in the Works Cited page.

2. Use in-text parenthetical citation to cite paraphrases or summaries. Any key phrases that you borrow word-for-word should go in quotation marks.

3. Cite opinions, interpretations, and results of original research.

4. In general, do not cite statements of widely accepted fact; but when following a source closely, cite it even if the material is widely accepted fact. If you are unsure if something is a "widely accepted fact," then you should probably cite it. See your instructor if you have any questions about facts.

Ways to Avoid Plagiarism

1. When in doubt, CITE! It can never hurt to over-cite or cite when you don't need to.

2. Give yourself plenty of time to research and write your essay, so that you do not feel pressured because a topic proves unworkable at the last minute. When writing a paper that uses sources, give yourself time to digest the research and synthesize your findings.

3. Take careful research notes that include full bibliographic citations. If you forget to write down the bibliographic data, you may be tempted not to bother with the citation.

4. Make it a habit to put parenthetical citations for all the sources you borrow from in each draft you write.

5. Keep a good documentation guide handy (i.e. your handbook) when you are doing your research and writing your paper.

6. Have confidence in yourself. Even the best writers are often unaware of their good ideas and think they have nothing to say when their writing says a lot. Original ideas come from working closely with the ideas of others, not from flashes of inspiration.

7. Know where to get help. Start with your instructor and ask questions about citations about which you are not sure. Besides your instructor, you can consult with a trained professional in the Writing Center (First Floor Chapman Hall, ex. 3131) for help with your writing. The reference librarians at McFarlin Library can help you with your research. The counselors at the Counseling Center (Alexander Health Center, ex. 2200) can help you with problems like time management, stress, and learning disabilities. Their services are confidential and free of charge. Finally, your academic advisor can help you put your course work in perspective.

Conclusion

Learning how to use sources is one of the most important things you will learn in college. By using sources well and by clearly indicating your debts to these sources, your writing gains authority, clarity, and precision. Writers who plagiarize lose the advantages of belonging to an intellectual discourse community (see "The Research Process" section for more information on this term). If plagiarizers are professionals, they may be barred from practicing their profession, or their work may not be taken seriously. If they are students, they not only may fail a course and be expelled from the University but will carry the stigma of having plagiarized. Instructors will be suspicious of their work and will be unwilling to support any of their future efforts, write recommendations for them, or even work with them at all. Plagiarism is one of the worst mistakes a writer can make. The best way to avoid it is to be scrupulous about citing quotations, paraphrases, and summaries from outside sources.

THE RESEARCH PROCESS

The following essay, taken from a guide very similar to this one at the University of Arizona, will give you a good idea why and how you will be doing research for essays you produce in Writing Program courses. In addition to defining terms such as "academic discourse" and "academic community," this essay also will help you distinguish between "academic" and "non-academic" sources, a skill which is a requirement of this program. It is reprinted with the permission of Burgess Publishing and the authors.

"THE PROCESS OF RESEARCH: JOINING THE CONVERSATION"

BY M.J. BRAUN AND SARAH PRINEAS

Why Do University Scholars Research?

University scholars not only make knowledge accessible to each new generation entering higher education, but they also work at developing new lines of inquiry and producing new knowledge in their various fields of study. This activity is known as scholarly research, and the ways of thinking, speaking, and writing that emerge from the act of research are often referred to as academic discourse. In The Philosophy of Literary Form, Kenneth Burke uses the metaphor of conversation to describe academic discourse:

> Imagine that you enter a parlor. You come late. When you arrive, others have long preceded you, and they are engaged in a heated discussion, too heated for them to pause and tell you exactly what it is about. In fact, the discussion had already begun long before any of them got there, so that no one present is qualified to retrace for you all the steps that had gone before. You listen for a while, until you decide that you have caught the tenor of the argument; then you put in your oar. Someone answers; you answer him; another comes to your defense; another aligns himself against you, to either the embarrassment or gratification of your opponent, depending upon the quality of your ally's assistance. However, the discussion is interminable. The hour grows late, You must depart. And you do depart, with the discussion still vigorously in progress. (110-11)

Because these academic conversations have been going on, as Burke says, "interminably," a scholar cannot expect to join them until she has done some research. Once the scholar has situated herself in the ongoing conversation through research and reading, she will be ready to become an active "speaker" in that conversation. In order to produce new knowledge, she considers what has been left out of the academic conversation. She asks, "What questions need to be raised? What arguments need to be made? What issues have been left unexamined?" Once she has found such a site for further argument, the scholar continues her research. Most scholars pursue a particular line of inquiry throughout their lives. Over the years, they develop theories about the phenomena they have researched, resulting in the production of new knowledge. This knowledge is often developed in opposition to previously held theories.

Because the scholar conducts research in this way, her work follows certain conventions. For example, she will cite authoritative sources to give her own work academic *ethos,* or credibility, in the eyes of scholarly readers. Second, she conducts research in order to sustain the conversation within her own work so that the other voices who have spoken on her issue can be heard speaking within her own work. Because sustaining this conversation is so important to scholars, they also value proper citation format for quotations and paraphrasing and always include an accurate record of sources—a bibliography or works cited. By including citations and a bibliography, the scholar makes it possible for the next person who picks up the conversation to become well informed on the issue by going back and studying the works cited.

How Do Scholars Decide upon a Topic?

Before starting research, it is important to be aware that in the university scholars choose topics that have relevance to the academic community. Topics for research do not begin and end with unexamined personal biases, because scholars expect to have their assumptions challenged by the academic conversations in their disciplines. For students at the university, topics arise from class discussions and from class readings—from any class, not just English composition. Beginning scholars and researchers need to become aware of the conflicts in their classrooms: What issues are under debate? What are scholars arguing about? What terms do different groups define in different ways? For example, English majors become aware that there is extensive debate about the "canon," or the list of texts considered by some scholars to be "authentic" literature. Some scholars insist that the traditionally assigned texts by revered authors—Chaucer, Shakespeare, Milton, Johnson, Dickens, or T. S. Eliot—must remain required materials. Other scholars working from different theories and assumptions call attention to the fact that the authors just mentioned represent a limited literary tradition that privileges the work of middle- and upper-class European males and insist that the canon must be expanded to include works previously not considered to be literature because of the gender, sexual orientation, religion, or ethnic or racial background of its authors. A novice scholar, for example, might explore the canon debate, analyze the arguments put forth by each player in the debate, and conclude by making an informed argument. Here's another example: In the medical field, nursing students and professors may be concerned about the issue of euthanasia and the role they should play as professionals within that debate. Other disciplines have other hot issues about which scholars argue. These are the sites where established assumptions have been called into question, and these questions are up for debate.

What Research Methods Do Scholars Use?

Less experienced researchers who are just entering the scholarly conversation should be careful not to jump to hasty conclusions, because they need to follow their research where it leads. That way they can leave their options open, allowing possibilities for new arguments to arise from the research. Often, novice researchers have been taught to find bits and pieces of texts that will fit smoothly into the argument they already want to make, glancing quickly through articles, circling only those quotations which support their previously determined position, and dismissing views which contradict their own. They may not consider the possibility that they might want to revise their original argument because the issue has broader implications than they had realized.

Experienced researchers approach research as a necessary step *before* participating in the scholarly conversations occurring in their disciplines. They realize the need to read first, to keep an open mind as they read, and to revise their original assumptions in the face of new knowledge. They recognize the complexity of issues and thus do not claim to have simple answers to complicated problems. Scholars generally respect opposing views because they know that issues can be approached in varied ways and that one can learn a great deal from other approaches, even those that challenge one's own assumptions. Experienced researchers keep careful track of their sources and evidence because they know they may have to give a careful accounting of their evidence if their conclusions or reasoning is challenged. Finally, scholars are aware that research takes time; they do not expect to complete their research in *one* trip to the library.

For example, as English 101 student Guy Natale began working on his academic project, he decided that as an aerospace and mechanical engineering major he wanted to research the military's use of unmanned aerial vehicles. Unlike most novice researchers, though, Natale did not begin his research with a set thesis in mind. As his instructor relates,

> While conducting his research Guy stumbled upon a topic that needed to be pursued further. Most of Guy's research in the beginning of the assignment centered on finding out how unmanned aerial vehicles (UAVs) are made and what they are used for, but as he slowly became an expert on UAVs, he realized that he did not approve of their potential use as weapons-bearing vehicles in warfare. Guy did not come upon this argument in a professional journal or read it in the newspaper; instead he developed his ideas about the ethical use of UAVs in conjunction with his research. At the rime he wrote his essay, these little, computer-controlled crafts were not being used to deliver missiles, but Guy could sense that this would be the next step. He proceeded to research and write a position paper that had a complex purpose: the goal was to take a stand against using unmanned aerial vehicles as weapon delivery systems and also to reaffirm the horrific nature of war by pointing out some of humanity's past mistakes.

How Does One Define a Topic?

Once students have begun to identify an area of inquiry—say, for example, the canon debate in English literature, or the euthanasia controversy among health professionals—it is time for them to learn more about the history of the issue, the players involved in the debate, and the kinds of argument's that are being deployed in the debate. The best way to go about this is to begin by visiting the library's computerized catalog of holdings. The first search through this database will be most effective if students approach the task with the attitude that they are engaging in play—they are exploring, searching for useful terms, following promising leads, getting ready to enter the stacks where the books and journals are waiting for them. After they've written down some call numbers, they will be ready to explore the library to track down the sources themselves. When they get to the stacks and find the book they were searching for, they should sit down right there and leaf through the book. They check the table of contents, the index, and the bibliography. They evaluate the chapter or essay titles, skim the introduction and conclusion, and figure out what type of source they have in front of them. They decide right there whether the book might be useful. If it is, they take a look at the shelf where they found that book and examine some of the nearby texts. By browsing the stacks and exploring texts in this way, they begin to get a feel for the debate they are researching. Possibly, certain names will appear several times—these are the players in the debate, the people engaged in the continuing argument. After checking the publication dates of each text, they begin to get a sense of the history of the debate. After reading a few introductions, the positions (rather than rhetorical choices) of those involved in .the debate will become more evident.

How Does One Evaluate Sources?

As scholars assemble research material, they are aware that there is a hierarchy of credibility among sources. This section analyzes the difference between scholarly and non-scholarly texts.

What Is A Scholarly Text?

A scholarly text is distinguished by the fact that the author makes evident in the text that he or she is making an argument as part of a continuing conversation. The author does so through literature reviews, bibliographies or works cited, footnotes or endnotes, and indexes. In other words, scholarly texts make the other voices—the voices of scholars who have previously written or spoken about the issue— "heard" and therefore present in the text. In non-scholarly texts, usually only the voice of the author can be heard.

Some examples of scholarly texts can include the: following:

> *Singly and collaboratively authored books:* These scholarly texts contribute something that has not been argued before in a scholarly conversation. These new arguments always build on knowledge that came before: sometimes they take an oppositional stance to that previous knowledge; sometimes they examine previously unconsidered aspects of the argument. Scholarly books are most often published by university, not commercial, presses. Books are published only after they have undergone a rigorous peer-review process. A panel of experts reviews the book to ensure that the author has a thorough understanding of the scope of the scholarly conversation; however, the panel does not evaluate the veracity of the argument. Scholarly works that have undergone this review process are considered credible sources among academics.

Be aware that some books may seem to follow these scholarly conventions, yet their credibility is non-existent in the academic community. For example, in *The Bell Curve: Intelligence and Class Structure* in *American Life* by Richard J. Herrnstein and Charles A. Murray, the authors argue that intelligence levels, not environmental circumstances, poverty, or lack of education, explain many of our social problems. In making their argument, the authors assert that intelligence is biologically, not environmentally, determined, and based on their data, they find that blacks are less intelligent than whites or Asians. The book *seems* to follow academic conventions, is written by two Harvard professors, is well documented, and acknowledges the theories on which the authors rely. Yet despite its semblance of credibility, as soon as the book came out scholars across the country, including scholars from Harvard, began to make academic arguments against it, questioning its use of evidence, the authors' manipulation of data, and the authors' suspect conclusions. Geneticists, biologists, and social scientists have challenged the book's premises, pointing out that the authors never clearly define "race," and, referring to the body of knowledge in their various disciplines, arguing the premise that race is in fact socially constructed. According to academic standards, *The Bell Curve* may seem to be a credible text; however, experts in many fields have rigorously questioned its "truth."

One thing to remember when reading scholarly texts is that the introductory chapter usually presents a concise over-view of the author's central argument. The introduction often contains a literature review (a review of the major *voices* in the conversation whose purpose is to review and then problematize what has been said before).

> *Journal articles:* An academic journal, by definition, contains articles relevant to a specific discipline. Journal articles, authored singly or collaboratively, do the same work as a book, in the sense that they are scholarly texts that present an argument and participate in the scholarly conversation. Before an article can be published in an academic journal, it must be refereed, which means that it has been reviewed by a panel of scholars expert in that field. The panel reviews the article to ensure that the author has a thorough understanding of the scope of the conversation; however the panel does not evaluate the veracity of the argument. Note that while journals are usually found in hard-copy format, they are increasingly appearing in online format.

An example of a journal article is R. G. Newby and D. E. Newby's "'The Bell Curve' Another Chapter in the Continuing Political Economy of Racism," which appeared in *American Behavioral Scientist* in 1995. The authors critique Herrnstein and Murray's *The Bell Curve: Intelligence and Class Structure in American Life* as part of their argument about the role that intellectuals have played in different historical periods in producing knowledge about intelligence and race. They argue that such pseudoscientific arguments about race arise under certain political and economic conditions. Therefore, for Newby and Newby, Herrnstein and Murray's "data" are less important than the political and economic conditions in which their book was produced.

Anthologies: Anthologies are collections of scholarly writings about a common subject. The materials published in anthologies are edited by scholars in a field. The articles republished in anthologies usually appeared first in academic journals or at academic conferences. Anthologies have a theme; all of the articles address some specific topic within the field. *Current Problems in Sociobiology* is an example of an anthology of academic papers presented at a conference at Cambridge University in 1980. The theme of this particular anthology, obviously, revolves around problems facing scholars engaged in sociobiological research.

What Is A Textbook?

While scholarly work seeks to produce new knowledge, textbooks construct a canon of knowledge, in the sense that they present previously theorized knowledge as information that is "true" without interrogating that "truth." In other words, textbooks do not employ the conventions of scholarly writing, because scholars always interrogate "truths." Because a textbook usually presents knowledge as, essentially, dead information, the conversation ends. At the same time, textbooks often come out in new editions in order to update the knowledge contained within, as the conversations have continued.

What Is A Non-academic Text?

Non-scholarly texts are intended for a general, or popular, audience. While scholarly texts make evident their participation in a conversation, non-academic texts derive their authority from a huge range of sources—from scholarly work, to received knowledge, to ideology. In this sense, non-academic texts are problematic because the theoretical assumptions in the texts are less evident and require a more actively analytical and knowledgeable reader. One problem with non-academic sources is that novice readers lack the analytical skills to recognize whether the theoretical assumptions underlying the text are credible, sometimes to the extent that anything that appears in print may seem credible. In non-scholarly texts, only the voice of the author is heard, while other voices—the voices of scholars who have previously written or spoken about the issue—are usually not present in the text. In academic texts, the voices of other participants in the conversation can be heard.

Singly and collaboratively authored books. These non-academic texts don't make a scholarly argument; their theoretical assumptions are either unexamined or buried. For example, in *You Just Don't Understand: Women and Men in Conversation,* author Deborah Tannen, writing for a popular audience, argues that men's and women's conversational styles differ. In this book, she presents numerous examples from men's and women's speech to illustrate her point; however, Tannen does not explicitly refer to the large body of linguistic theory which informs her analysis. In her scholarly work on the same subject, *Gender and Discourse,* Tannen supports her method of analysis by citing the linguistic theory that informs it. Non-academic texts pose a problem more for the uninformed than the informed reader because those readers who are, in this case, unfamiliar with linguistics are unaware of the author's knowledge of linguistics itself and her standing as a scholar in that field. A reader unfamiliar with conventions of academic texts has no way of knowing if a book by Deborah Tannen on gender and conversation is more credible than a book by Oprah Winfrey on the same subject.

Oprah Winfrey might have interesting things to say about the differences in men's and women's conversational styles, but her observations would not be based on accepted linguistic theory or current research, but rather on passively received ideas. For example, according to linguistic theory, gender differences in conversational styles arc explained as socially, not biologically, contingent. On the other hand, a non-linguist may recognize that there are gender differences in conversation styles but attribute these differences to testosterone rather than the social roles men and women play.

Anthologies. Non-academic anthologies are collections of popular rather than scholarly writings about a common subject. The materials published in popular anthologies are not necessarily edited by scholars and usually appeared first in popular sources such as books, newspapers, or magazines. An example of a non-academic anthology is *The Bell Curve Wars: Race, Intelligence, and the Future of America,* edited by Steven Fraser, containing articles written by scholars for a popular audience. The anthology contains many articles arguing against the claims made by sociologists Herrnstein and Murray in *The Bell Curve: Intelligence and Class Structure in American Life,* including articles by biologist Stephen Jay Gould and literary theorist Henry Louis Gates Jr. These articles are not scholarly in that Gould, for example, does not write for an audience of biologists, but for a more general audience interested in the debate.

Magazines. may seem to provide current information, but they are generally not considered by scholars to be reliable sources. Often, they do not acknowledge their sources, as scholars do, and they are usually not aimed at an academic audience. Magazine articles may even be authored by someone nor trained to speak on the subject. For example, a magazine reporter has been trained in journalism, not the subject about which he or she is writing.

Newspapers. Newspaper articles have the same limitations for scholarly use as magazine articles. Reporters, rather than scholars, usually but not always write the articles. Because sources for newspaper articles are unacknowledged, there is no way of knowing what sources are informing a reporter's version of events.

Web pages. In the hierarchy of credibility, Web pages arc less credible than print or hard-copy texts for a variety of reasons: anyone (not necessarily an "expert" or scholar) can publish a Web page; Web pages are ephemeral (that is, they can be revised without warning, unlike print sources); sometimes the organizations that publish Web pages can construct the site in such a way that it seems "official" and credible, when in fact it is not. In addition, the Web itself was originally developed by the military and adopted for commercial purposes. Therefore, the format and content of the Web may serve hidden purposes outside of scholarly inquiry. Recently, some scholarly journals have begun to publish on the Web and follow all of the conventions of hard-copy journals.

Works Cited

Burke, Kenneth. *The Philosophy of Literary Form.* Baton Rouge: Louisiana State UP, 1941

Current Problems in Sociobiology. Ed. King's College Sociobiology Group. New York: Cambridge UP, 1982.

Fraser, Steven, ed. *The Bell Curve Wars: Race, Intelligence, and the Future of America.* New York: Bask, 1995.

Herrnstein, Richard J., and Charles A. Murray. *The Bell Curve: Intelligence and Class Structure in American Life.* New York: Free, 1994.

Newby, Robert, and Diane Newby. "'The Bell Curve'—Another Chapter in the Continuing Political Economy of Racism." *American Behavioral Scientist* 39 (1995): 12-24.

Tannen, Deborah. *You Just Don't Understand: Women and Men in Conversation.* New York: Morrow, 1990.

Research Resources

Where to Begin? There are many ways to begin a research project, but the previous section, "The Process of Research," suggested that you begin your research by visiting the library's computerized catalogue of holdings. You can do this at TU either on campus or off through the internet by entering <http://www.lib.utulsa.edu/> into the address bar of your web browser. No matter

> For more information on how to use library databases, to create search terms, and to evaluate web sites, see your writing handbook, Diana Hacker's *Rules for Writers*.

what Writing Program course you are currently taking, we strongly suggest that you take this advice and begin with either the library's electronic catalogue or its list of research databases, rather than, say, an internet search through Google. We'll explain why shortly. For now, suffice it to say that the library's databases will more quickly lead you to the kind of reliable and authoritative sources required by most college courses.

The most powerful place to start any research project is by using the library's vast collection of databases. Access this list of databases from the library website by following this procedure:
1. Click on "Articles and Databases" in the menu of the library's home web site.
2. On the next page, you will see a box entitled "Advanced Guides."
3. Click on "English/Literature."

You'll notice that from the list of Advance Guides that you can use this site to research any topic in any class. For example, if you are in a First Seminar course, you might select the discipline that most closely reflects the topic of your course, say, "History." If you are in ENGL 3003, you might select "Engineering" or "Nursing." Also look at the Quick Guides for your field as well.

Once you select a subject, a new page will come up. On this page will be listed all the databases that are relevant to that field. In the field of English language and literature, for example, there are many databases. Some of the most important include Academic Search Complete, Project Muse, JSTOR, and the MLA International Bibliography. The latter database indexes every scholarly publication, from book to article, published in the field of modern languages and literatures. As you might guess, this is a very important resource for anyone doing a research paper on literature. The MLA bibliography is not a completely full-text database, however, so you might have to find the actual item you are looking for in the library catalogue or through a full-text database like JSTOR.

On the English library database page, you will also find other relevant databases, such as the TU Library catalog where you can find books on your subject, links to full-text databases, and links to reference material. At the bottom of the page, the librarians have placed a link to their "English Language and Literature Research Guide," which contains much useful information on writing a research paper for English class, especially 1033. You will learn more about these resources during your required library orientation in ENGL 1033.

Although not all sources found through the library's web page are academic, by beginning with that page, you are better assured that you are getting reliable information that will fit the academic source requirements of many English courses. When you do a search of the internet using a search engine, you have no way of knowing whether the information you are getting is reliable or authoritative. Although it may sound counter-intuitive, you are getting a much broader range of different kinds of information through the library's web page than you could doing a Google search. This is because the library concentrates mostly on *academic* sources, the kind you will be required to have in many of your courses. (See "The Research Process" for a definition of "academic sources").

Although your instructors in class and the librarians during orientation will go into more detail on how to conduct research in an academic discourse community, here are a few helpful hints and reminders for you as you begin:

- **Start with the library's webpage.** This is the gateway to most of the information you will need for a college research project.

- **Evaluate web sources carefully.** If you must use an internet search engine to search for sources, examine each page carefully to assess its authority and reliability. See *Rules for Writers* for the chapter on evaluating web site sources. If you are not sure of a web page's credibility ask your instructor or email him/her the URL.

- **Keep good records.** Write down the information you'll need for your Works Cited page (and write it in the proper format—it'll be good practice for your papers). Print out or make copies of articles that you know you'll be using; if you need something from them, there isn't the risk that the journal is checked out or the server is down when you really need it.

- **Bibliographies.** Look in the bibliography of one source to find other sources relevant to your topic. Once you find a few, you might notice that they often refer to some of the same sources. You are now starting to see what "discourse community" really means. Additionally, some disciplines publish entire books that are bibliographies on a specific topic, and these provide invaluable resources. Most of these can be found in the stacks along with other books.

- **Ask a Librarian.** Librarians are specially trained to help you use the library's resources to their fullest. They may not know exactly what sources you may need for a research project in a particular discipline (that is the job of your professor), but they will certainly know *where* and *how* you can access the information you need. Of course, they will not do your research for you, but you should take advantage of their knowledge and expertise.

The University of Tulsa Writing Program

A note on MLA style and its importance

Many courses in The Writing Program at the University of Tulsa require you to do research, and doing research requires that you cite your sources. In our 1000-level writing courses like ENGL 1033, we ask that you use a citation system known as the MLA style in your papers. MLA stands for the Modern Language Association, which is the largest organized body of people who work in the fields of languages and literatures. There are many styles available to different disciplines, such as the Chicago style for journalism or the APA for psychology, but the Writing Program uses MLA because it is the style that those of us in the Writing Program faculty are most familiar. We use it in our own work in the discipline of English language and literature and are thus best equipped to teach it. By learning one system in depth, you learn what citations systems in general require you to do to properly give credit to others, which is a skill that you can transfer to any discipline. *Note: In other courses, you may be asked to used styles other than the MLA—ask your professor or librarian for more information on the required style.*

However, the most important reason for using any documentation style is academic honesty. Plagiarism, the unauthorized use of someone else's work, is an issue that you will be asked to think about repeatedly through your academic career (see the "Plagiarism Statement" section for more information). It is a serious and grave offense and one for which MLA sytle is designed to help avert. That is, by using proper citation, listing all of the sources of your information, you will be able to avoid inadvertently plagiarizing and misappropriating research done by other people.

MLA style is easy to understand and simple to use. In fact, it is one of the most efficient and streamlined of all the citation styles because, rather than footnotes, it uses in-text parenthetical citation to give page numbers and just enough information that you can locate the item in the Works Cited page. From the Works Cited page, then, anyone should be able to look up your sources (Gibaldi). For the most complete explanation of MLA style, we strongly suggest that you buy the *MLA Handbook for Writers of Research Papers*, which is offered as an optional text in the bookstore. Your grammar handbook also has a short section on MLA style. In addition to what may be found in your writing handbooks, the library, writing center, book store, and many other facilities on campus can help you learn how to use MLA. Your instructors will deal with documentation in class, and they will surely help you if you have questions.

A good rule to keep in mind is "When in doubt, cite." Moreover, attempted but mistaken documentation is always better than no documentation at all. Titles and names placed in the wrong order on a works cited page, or, too much information given within the paper will always save you from being accused of academic dishonesty. Unlike many other fields, in the academic realm ideas are our only currency and our only gauge of good work. They are available for use by any who will use them so long as credit is given where credit is due. It is worth your time to make sure to document every source. Please learn to use MLA and to use it to the best of your ability. It will save you many problems in the future.

How to Write an In-class Essay

Writing an in-class, timed essay is a critical skill on which you will be assessed in your first-year writing course at the University of Tulsa. If you are in ENGL 1033, a sample of your in-class writing will serve as a vital component of your portfolio because it demonstrates your ability to recall information, synthesize readings, argue coherently, and think critically under pressure. It also serves to measure your readiness to take college-level essay exams that will be required of you in more advanced classes.

In ENGL 1033, all in-class writing assignments are timed at exactly 45 minutes, but in other writing courses, the time could vary. At any rate, one of the best ways to prepare for an in-class essay is to practice taking one: Set aside the same time limit that you will be given in class and then attempt to answer a practice question that you, a classmate, or your professor has given you. Being familiar with the testing situation is half the battle for succeeding at any timed test.

By following a planned process, you can increase your chances of success on an in-class writing assignment. Consider using this step-by-step guide (or your own variation on it) to make the most of your writing time:

1. **Read** the question carefully. Make sure you understand what it is asking—look for key words that suggest a possible approach (for example, if it asks "why" then a causal argument might be in order).
2. Take 5-10 min. to **prewrite** on a separate sheet of paper. Brainstorm some ideas, generate a thesis, and scribble out an outline. If you have an outline to follow, you'll be less likely to get off topic.
3. On the top of a new sheet, write out your **thesis**. To make sure you are answering the question, repeat key words and phrases from the question. DO NOT write an intro yet—your thesis will serve as an intro for now—the body paragraphs are the most important because that is where your evidence is. Keep the thesis page where you can see it so that you are constantly tying your evidence back to it.
4. Use a separate sheet of paper for each **paragraph**. Start with the easiest body paragraph first, then go to harder ones. By putting paragraphs on separate pages, you can shuffle the order later. Make sure each body paragraph has at least one good, concrete example and an interpretation of that example. State reasons and assumptions where necessary. The body is the heart of your essay and worth the most points, so make sure you have at least three good body paragraphs.
5. Write a **conclusion** that sums up your points and leaves the reader with a good idea of why you made your argument to a particular discourse community. Answer the question "So What"?
6. If you have time, go back to the thesis page and write an **intro** under your thesis. Use your intro to contextualize your thesis in the ongoing debate or conversation in the discourse community that your class is a part of.
7. Save a few minutes for **revision and proofreading**. Add extra support where you need it. Make sure there are no major errors.

This process is based on the assumption that you ***know the material*** you are being tested over and that you have gotten a good night's rest and a balanced meal before the exam (don't laugh—they're important factors). If you have issues with performance or test-taking anxiety visit CSAS (see "Campus Writing Resources" section) and refer to the TU "Handbook: College Experience" (Wilson).

ORAL PRESENTATION GUIDE

It falls upon the Writing Program at The University of Tulsa to introduce you to the basic skills of oral presentations in an academic setting. An oral presentation consists of a student delivering material aloud to his or her classmates in the classroom and is required in all ENGL 1033 sections and may be required in other writing courses as well.

The topic, format, and length of oral presentations can vary from section to section, but many of the basic criteria for a good presentation are the same for a good written essay or portfolio. Considering your audience, for example, is key to a successful presentation. Knowing who your audience is, as well as what they know, can guide your decisions about what to put in and what to leave out of your presentation. By knowing your audience, you will know what kind of language to use, at what level to "pitch" your presentation.

Other important aspects of oral presentation that you may want to consider:

- **Purpose**: What are you trying to do with your presentation? What are the goals of the assignment? How will your presentation meet those goals?

- **Voice**: Are you speaking clearly and projecting your voice? Can everyone hear you? Presentations that are not read are often the most effective because reading voices tend to get monotonous. If you must read, make sure that your voice is dynamic and that you don't read too fast.

- **Media Aids**: What part of your presentation would be more effective in visual or audio form? That may be as simple as a handout or as sophisticated as a Power Point Presentation with embedded multimedia.

- **Conciseness**: Make sure that both the spoken and visual parts of your presentation are on topic and to the point. In visual aids, condense the spoken material to key words or phrases so that your audience will remember it rather than read it along with you.

- **Repetition**: Because your audience is listening to you, rather than reading your presentation on the page, repeat key points, terms, and phrases so that they will remember the information.

- **Eye Contact**: Try to make eye contact with your audience—not just as a group—but as individuals. Even if you read your presentation, you should often glance up and look at your audience.

- **Appearance**: In academic settings, as well as corporate ones, presenters often try to look as professionally as possible, and those standards may depend upon the industry. Typically, presenters do not wear what they would normally to class or around the house.

We also recommend that you practice your presentation before you give it. Recite it in front of a roommate or a mirror to get the timing down and to fine tune exactly how you want to say things. This may sound like a hassle, but many professionals do the same thing before important presentations.

Lastly, remember to pay attention to what your instructor asks of you in your presentation. Grading criteria can vary widely from instructor to instructor. If you are confused or have concerns, please ask.

APPENDICES

These appendices contain documents that you will need during <u>each</u> of your writing courses. As you will notice, the pages are perforated so that, when necessary, you may tear out the pages to turn in to your instructor. They include:

- Plagiarism Statement Acknowledgement Form (4)
- A Standard Release Form (4)
- Freshman Essay Contest Entry Form
- Nomination Outstanding Teacher & Tutor Awards

There are several copies of a few of the documents because you will need to use a new one in each of your writing classes.

Therefore, as with your writing handbook, we recommend that you keep this guide throughout your career at TU.

THE UNIVERSITY OF TULSA WRITING PROGRAM

PLAGIARISM STATEMENT ACKNOWLEDGEMENT FORM

This acknowledgement provides confirmation that the Plagiarism Statement has been read, discussed, and understood by All Students in ENGL 1004, 1033, and 3003.

Student Name and ID Number: _____

Course Name and Number: _____

Section Number: _____ **Semester and Year:** _____

Instructor: _____ **Time:** _____
(Please Print)   last name   first name

To Students: By signing this form, you confirm that you understand what plagiarism is, that you know the policies that pertain to plagiarism , and that you accept responsibility for any plagiarism in your work.

To Instructors: All students in your section [s] should read the entire plagiarism policy of the Writing Program and sign this form **at least one time** during their writing course work at The University of Tulsa. All students who did not take these courses at T.U. should read the statement and sign the form. For students who have already read the statement in a previous class, you should reiterate the highlights of the statement and ask them to sign the form as a reminder of their responsibility to adhere to the policy.

Date Plagiarism Statement was discussed: _____

Instructor's Signature: _____

Student's Signature: _____ **Date:** _____

The University of Tulsa Writing Program

Plagiarism Statement Acknowledgement Form

This acknowledgement provides confirmation that the Plagiarism Statement has been read, discussed, and understood by All Students in ENGL 1004, 1033, and 3003.

Student Name and ID Number: _____

Course Name and Number: _____

Section Number: _____ **Semester and Year:** _____

Instructor: _____ **Time:** _____
(Please Print)   last name   first name

To Students: By signing this form, you confirm that you understand what plagiarism is,
that you know the policies that pertain to plagiarism , and that you accept responsibility for any plagiarism in your work.

To Instructors: All students in your section [s] should read the entire plagiarism policy
of the Writing Program and sign this form **at least one time** during their writing course work at The University of Tulsa. All students who did not take these courses at T.U. should read the statement and sign the form. For students who have already read the statement in a previous class, you should reiterate the highlights of the statement and ask them to sign the form as a reminder of their responsibility to adhere to the policy.

Date Plagiarism Statement was discussed: _____

Instructor's Signature: _____

Student's Signature: _____ **Date:** _____

The University of Tulsa Writing Program

Plagiarism Statement Acknowledgement Form

This acknowledgement provides confirmation that the Plagiarism Statement has been read, discussed, and understood by All Students in ENGL 1004, 1033, and 3003.

Student Name and ID Number: _____

Course Name and Number: _____

Section Number: _____ **Semester and Year:** _____

Instructor: _____ **Time:** _____
(Please Print)   last name   first name

To Students: By signing this form, you confirm that you understand what plagiarism is, that you know the policies that pertain to plagiarism , and that you accept responsibility for any plagiarism in your work.

To Instructors: All students in your section [s] should read the entire plagiarism policy of the Writing Program and sign this form **at least one time** during their writing course work at The University of Tulsa. All students who did not take these courses at T.U. should read the statement and sign the form. For students who have already read the statement in a previous class, you should reiterate the highlights of the statement and ask them to sign the form as a reminder of their responsibility to adhere to the policy.

Date Plagiarism Statement was discussed: _____

Instructor's Signature: _____

Student's Signature: _____ **Date:** _____

THE UNIVERSITY OF TULSA WRITING PROGRAM

PLAGIARISM STATEMENT ACKNOWLEDGEMENT FORM

This acknowledgement provides confirmation that the Plagiarism Statement has been read, discussed, and understood by All Students in ENGL 1004, 1033, and 3003.

Student Name and ID Number: _____

Course Name and Number: _____

Section Number: _____ **Semester and Year:** _____

Instructor: _____ **Time:** _____
(Please Print)   last name   first name

To Students: By signing this form, you confirm that you understand what plagiarism is,
   that you know the policies that pertain to plagiarism , and that you accept responsibility for any
   plagiarism in your work.

To Instructors: All students in your section [s] should read the entire plagiarism policy
   of the Writing Program and sign this form **at least one time** during their writing course work at
   The University of Tulsa. All students who did not take these courses at T.U. should read the statement and sign the form. For students who have already read the statement in a previous class, you
   should reiterate the highlights of the statement and ask them to sign the form as a reminder of their
   responsibility to adhere to the policy.

Date Plagiarism Statement was discussed: _____

Instructor's Signature: _____

Student's Signature: _____ **Date:** _____

University of Tulsa Writing Program

Standard Release Form

Sample student papers often are used in universities for faculty development sessions and other purposes. You are being asked for your permission to use copies of the papers you produce throughout this semester. Your decision on whether to allow the use of your papers will **not** in any way affect your grade.

Course Information

Semester: _____   Year: _____

Title: _____
(*e.g.*, Exposition and Argumentation)

Catalog Number: _____
(*e.g.*, ENGL 1033)

Section Number: _____

Teaching Portfolio

Your instructor maintains a teaching portfolio that serves as a record of the instructor's teaching and that may be used in hiring decisions (internally and with other universities), in promotion decisions, and in faculty-development situations. The portfolio includes sample student papers. Place your initials beside your response:

_____   I give permission for the use of my papers in my instructor's teaching portfolio.

_____   I give permission for the use of my papers *anonymously* in my instructor's teaching portfolio.

_____   I prefer that *none* of my papers appear in my instructor's teaching portfolio.

Faculty-Development Sessions

The university faculty often hold sessions to discuss grading and assignment criteria, and student papers are used in these situations. Place your initials beside your response:

_____   I give permission for the use of my papers in faculty-development sessions (grading calibration exercises, discussion of assignment criteria/problems, etc.).

_____   I give permission for the use of my papers *anonymously* in faculty-development sessions (grading calibration exercises, discussion of assignment criteria/problems, etc.).

_____   I prefer that *none* of my papers be used in any faculty-development sessions.

Future Classes

Instructors sometimes use former students' papers to illustrate writing skills/problems in current classes. Place your initials beside your response:

_____   I give permission for the use of my papers in future classes as examples of student writing.

_____   I give permission for the use of my papers *anonymously* in future classes as examples of student writing.

_____   I prefer that *none* of my papers be used in future classes.

Accreditation

For accreditation purposes, the university periodically must submit samples of student work to be reviewed by committees not affiliated with the university. Place your initials beside your response:

_____   I give permission for the use of my papers for accreditation purposes.

_____   I give permission for the use of my papers *anonymously* for accreditation purposes.

_____   I prefer that *none* of my papers be used for accreditation purposes.

Student Information

First Name: _____   Last Name: _____

I.D. Number: _____

Signature: _____   Date: _____

University of Tulsa Writing Program

Standard Release Form

Sample student papers often are used in universities for faculty development sessions and other purposes. You are being asked for your permission to use copies of the papers you produce throughout this semester. Your decision on whether to allow the use of your papers will **not** in any way affect your grade.

Course Information

Semester: _____   Year: _____

Title: _____
(e.g., Exposition and Argumentation)

Catalog Number: _____
(e.g., ENGL 1033)

Section Number: _____

Teaching Portfolio

Your instructor maintains a teaching portfolio that serves as a record of the instructor's teaching and that may be used in hiring decisions (internally and with other universities), in promotion decisions, and in faculty-development situations. The portfolio includes sample student papers. Place your initials beside your response:

_____   I give permission for the use of my papers in my instructor's teaching portfolio.

_____   I give permission for the use of my papers *anonymously* in my instructor's teaching portfolio.

_____   I prefer that *none* of my papers appear in my instructor's teaching portfolio.

Faculty-Development Sessions

The university faculty often hold sessions to discuss grading and assignment criteria, and student papers are used in these situations. Place your initials beside your response:

_____   I give permission for the use of my papers in faculty-development sessions (grading calibration exercises, discussion of assignment criteria/problems, etc.).

_____   I give permission for the use of my papers *anonymously* in faculty-development sessions (grading calibration exercises, discussion of assignment criteria/problems, etc.).

_____   I prefer that *none* of my papers be used in any faculty-development sessions.

Future Classes

Instructors sometimes use former students' papers to illustrate writing skills/problems in current classes. Place your initials beside your response:

_____   I give permission for the use of my papers in future classes as examples of student writing.

_____   I give permission for the use of my papers *anonymously* in future classes as examples of student writing.

_____   I prefer that *none* of my papers be used in future classes.

Accreditation

For accreditation purposes, the university periodically must submit samples of student work to be reviewed by committees not affiliated with the university. Place your initials beside your response:

_____   I give permission for the use of my papers for accreditation purposes.

_____   I give permission for the use of my papers *anonymously* for accreditation purposes.

_____   I prefer that *none* of my papers be used for accreditation purposes.

Student Information

First Name: _____   Last Name: _____

I.D. Number: _____

Signature: _____   Date: _____

UNIVERSITY OF TULSA WRITING PROGRAM

STANDARD RELEASE FORM

Sample student papers often are used in universities for faculty development sessions and other purposes. You are being asked for your permission to use copies of the papers you produce throughout this semester. Your decision on whether to allow the use of your papers will **not** in any way affect your grade.

> **Course Information**
>
> Semester: _____ Year: _____
> Title: _____
> (*e.g.*, Exposition and Argumentation)
>
> Catalog Number: _____
> (*e.g.*, ENGL 1033)
>
> Section Number: _____

Teaching Portfolio
Your instructor maintains a teaching portfolio that serves as a record of the instructor's teaching and that may be used in hiring decisions (internally and with other universities), in promotion decisions, and in faculty-development situations. The portfolio includes sample student papers. Place your initials beside your response:

_____ I give permission for the use of my papers in my instructor's teaching portfolio.
_____ I give permission for the use of my papers *anonymously* in my instructor's teaching portfolio.
_____ I prefer that *none* of my papers appear in my instructor's teaching portfolio.

Faculty-Development Sessions
The university faculty often hold sessions to discuss grading and assignment criteria, and student papers are used in these situations. Place your initials beside your response:

_____ I give permission for the use of my papers in faculty-development sessions (grading calibration exercises, discussion of assignment criteria/problems, etc.).
_____ I give permission for the use of my papers *anonymously* in faculty-development sessions (grading calibration exercises, discussion of assignment criteria/problems, etc.).
_____ I prefer that *none* of my papers be used in any faculty-development sessions.

Future Classes
Instructors sometimes use former students' papers to illustrate writing skills/problems in current classes. Place your initials beside your response:

_____ I give permission for the use of my papers in future classes as examples of student writing.
_____ I give permission for the use of my papers *anonymously* in future classes as examples of student writing.
_____ I prefer that *none* of my papers be used in future classes.

Accreditation
For accreditation purposes, the university periodically must submit samples of student work to be reviewed by committees not affiliated with the university. Place your initials beside your response:

_____ I give permission for the use of my papers for accreditation purposes.
_____ I give permission for the use of my papers *anonymously* for accreditation purposes.
_____ I prefer that *none* of my papers be used for accreditation purposes.

Student Information

First Name: _____ Last Name: _____

I.D. Number: _____

Signature: _____ Date: _____

UNIVERSITY OF TULSA WRITING PROGRAM

STANDARD RELEASE FORM

Sample student papers often are used in universities for faculty development sessions and other purposes. You are being asked for your permission to use copies of the papers you produce throughout this semester. Your decision on whether to allow the use of your papers will **not** in any way affect your grade.

> **Course Information**
>
> Semester: _____ Year: _____
>
> Title: _____
> (*e.g.*, Exposition and Argumentation)
>
> Catalog Number: _____
> (*e.g.*, ENGL 1033)
>
> Section Number: _____

Teaching Portfolio

Your instructor maintains a teaching portfolio that serves as a record of the instructor's teaching and that may be used in hiring decisions (internally and with other universities), in promotion decisions, and in faculty-development situations. The portfolio includes sample student papers. Place your initials beside your response:

_____ I give permission for the use of my papers in my instructor's teaching portfolio.

_____ I give permission for the use of my papers *anonymously* in my instructor's teaching portfolio.

_____ I prefer that *none* of my papers appear in my instructor's teaching portfolio.

Faculty-Development Sessions

The university faculty often hold sessions to discuss grading and assignment criteria, and student papers are used in these situations. Place your initials beside your response:

_____ I give permission for the use of my papers in faculty-development sessions (grading calibration exercises, discussion of assignment criteria/problems, etc.).

_____ I give permission for the use of my papers *anonymously* in faculty-development sessions (grading calibration exercises, discussion of assignment criteria/problems, etc.).

_____ I prefer that *none* of my papers be used in any faculty-development sessions.

Future Classes

Instructors sometimes use former students' papers to illustrate writing skills/problems in current classes. Place your initials beside your response:

_____ I give permission for the use of my papers in future classes as examples of student writing.

_____ I give permission for the use of my papers *anonymously* in future classes as examples of student writing.

_____ I prefer that *none* of my papers be used in future classes.

Accreditation

For accreditation purposes, the university periodically must submit samples of student work to be reviewed by committees not affiliated with the university. Place your initials beside your response:

_____ I give permission for the use of my papers for accreditation purposes.

_____ I give permission for the use of my papers *anonymously* for accreditation purposes.

_____ I prefer that *none* of my papers be used for accreditation purposes.

Student Information

First Name: _____ Last Name: _____

I.D. Number: _____

Signature: _____ Date: _____

UNIVERSITY OF TULSA WRITING PROGRAM

FRESHMAN ESSAY CONTEST ENTRY FORM

During the spring of the same academic year in which you were enrolled in ENGL 1033, you are eligible to enter the University Writing Program's annual Freshman Essay Contest. Submit one essay that critically addresses a text or texts used in your class. Winners will receive prizes and will be recognized at the awards ceremony in April.

Submission Requirements:
   *Typed, double-spaced
   *Conform to MLA guidelines (formatting and documentation)
   *Use your student ID on the essay instead of your name
   *Do not include your instructor's name on essay
   *Paperclip this submission form to your entry

Essays, along with this completed form, are due in the English Department office (Zink Hall 365) on or before the first Monday in April. For more information, contact Mrs. Sandy Vice at sandra-vice@utulsa.edu or 631-3557.

Full Name (please print): _____

ID number: _____

Telephone number: _____

Instructor Name: _____

UNIVERSITY OF TULSA WRITING PROGRAM

NOMINATION OUTSTANDING TEACHER & CONSULTANT AWARDS

(Teachers and consultants may be nominated by their students and/or colleagues).

Outstanding Teacher Award
Teaching Assistants who are instructors for ENGL 1004, 1033, or 3003 are eligible for the Outstanding Teacher Award if they have taught one of these courses in the Fall or Spring of this academic year and have not previously won the award.

Outstanding Consultant Award
Teaching Assistants who consult in The Writing Center in the Fall or Spring of this academic year are eligible for the Outstanding Consultant Award if they have not previously won it.

Please contact Sandra Vice at the number below to get a list of the eligible teachers and consultants.

I nominate_____of the TU Writing Program for the (circle one below)

           Outstanding Teacher Award   Outstanding Consultant Award

In the space below, describe briefly what qualifies your nominee for the above award. Please be specific as possible. Continue on the back of this form if necessary.

Name of nominator (please print) _____

Signature of nominator _____

Date: _____

Please seal this form in an envelope and drop it in the mailbox in the English Department office (Zink Hall 365—see Sandy Vice) by *the first Monday in April*. Direct any questions to Sandy Vice, ext. 2557 or sandra-vice@utulsa.edu

WORKS CITED

Braun, M.J. and Sarah Prineas. "First-Year Composition as an Introduction to Academic Discourse." In *Strategies for Teaching First-Year Composition.* Ed. Duane Rouen, et al. Ubana, IL: National Council of Teachers of English, 2002. 570-582.

Gibaldi, Joseph, ed. *MLA Handbook for Writers of Research Papers.* 7th ed. New York: Modern Language Association of America, 2009.

Reynolds, Nedra. *Portfolio Keeping.* New York: Bedford/St. Martin's, 2000.

Wilson, Lisa, et al. Handbook: College Experience. 2000. University of Tulsa. 2 March 2005 <http://www.personal.utulsa.edu/~robert-donaldson/handbook.htm#Study%20Skills>.